DARK DEVOURING

DARK DEVOURING

Songs from Magpie & Sun Mountain

Thomas McGuire

RAGGED SKY PRESS
Princeton, New Jersey

Copyright © 2024 by Thomas McGuire
Published by Ragged Sky Press
270 Griggs Drive
Princeton, NJ 08540
raggedsky.com
All Rights Reserved
ISBN: 978-1-933974-59-0
Library of Congress Control Number: 2024938583
This book has been composed in Adobe Garamond and Avenir Next
Text and cover design by Pamela Schnitter
Printed on acid-free paper. ∞
Printed in the United States of America

Magpie: n. A bird whose thievish disposition suggested to someone that it might be taught to talk.
   —AMBROSE BIERCE, *Devil's Dictionary*

magpie: v. (transitive, intransitive) to steal or hoard; (intransitive) to talk idly; (transitive) to mark with patches of black and white or light and dark.

Nobody sees a magpie—really—it is so strange it takes time—we haven't time—and to see takes time, like having a friend takes time.
   —MAGPIE RIFFING ON GEORGIA O'KEEFFE

Angelus Novus shows an angel looking as though he is about to move away from something he is fixedly contemplating. His eyes are staring, his mouth is open, his wings are spread. This is how one pictures the angel of history. His face is turned toward the past. Where we perceive a chain of events, he sees one single catastrophe which keeps piling wreckage upon wreckage and hurls it in front of his feet. The angel would like to stay, awaken the dead, and make whole what has been smashed.
   —WALTER BENJAMIN

CONTENTS

Du mußt dein Leben ändern   1

〰

Runic Riddle   4
Alexander Wilson's Essential Magpie   5
Snag Breac at Glendalough, Co. Wicklow   6
Magpie Rises Coming Down to Earth   8
The Bird Refused   10
On Seeing a Jakhodo Scroll Painting Entitled *Magpie (Village Spirit) & Tiger (Mountain Spirit)*   11

〰 〰

Feeder off Battlefields   14
A Ripe Rude Garden   19
Three Ways of Looking at Magpie—a Most Becoming Bird   20
Hunger   22
Like a Common Thief: Magpie Caught, Caged, Catalogued   23
Every Bone Must Find Its Fellow Bone   25
C.W. Peale's Recipe for Preserving Birds, &c,   27
Zebulon Pike Marvels at Magpies Scavenging in the Snow Shadow of Mt. Shavano   28
The Raising of the Dead   29

〰 〰 〰

Becoming Magpie   32
Haggis   34
Gertrude Stein on a Soul's Miraculous Migration to Magpiety   35
Holding Still, Becoming Magpie   36
The Girl in the Village   37

〰〰〰〰

A Prayer for T.H., My Magpie, & Me   40
Ubi Sunt   41
Rites of Passage at the Feast of Lupercal, 1973   42
Grief Observed   44
Ghorbân: a Poem of Sacrifice   46
Magpie Rues the Cherry Orchard   47
Perhaps One World. . . but Please Not One Word for Bird   48
Riddle Second   49
Annihilate Is an English Word   50

〰〰〰〰〰

A Scientist Marvels at Magpie Mob Tactics   54
Force, the Hero   56
Lizard Brain   59
Artemis Goes Hunting   63
Family Recipe   65
Endnotes (What I Didn't Write)   66
No More Story Time   69
Hansel Can't You See, Gretel's Got PTSD?   70
Sloe Gin, Slow Suicide   72
Heirloom Photograph   75
Heorot   78
Het Huis   79
Tonight My Father's Dying   81
Rust   82
Garden Plots   83
Peace Lily (with Peace Walls Leading to a Haiga)   85

〰〰〰〰〰〰

Magpie Sings on Sun Mountain   89

ACKNOWLEDGMENTS   105
NOTES   111
ILLUSTRATION CREDITS   116
ABOUT THE AUTHOR   117

Du mußt dein Leben ändern

(Proverbs Magpie Flies By)

you have to live another life
don the magpie mask and know
theft is the first duty of mankind

> if change your life you must
> sing then in multiplicity
> announce the many voices

pray, recycle every day
work and prayer are one,
be derivative, but only *incognito*

> converse daily with the dead
> rattle spirits beyond the burning lands
> raise their bones breath by breath

repeat this koan: *the spirit is a bone*
God speaks in stones and bones,
birds and trees... *the spirit is a bone*

> collect masks, words, pelvises, femurs
> change your voice each day,
> change it even in mid-sentence
>
> you must live another's life

What is magpiety? I shall never achieve
A magpie heart, a hairy nostril over the beak, a flight
That always renews just when coming down,
And so I shall never comprehend magpiety.

—CZESŁAW MIŁOSZ, "Magpiety"

Runic Riddle

I'm a bizarre bird with varied voices;
Audubon says my song is *queg* or *maag*,
But I can howl like a hound, bleat like a lamb
Honk like a honker, shriek like a shrike.
At times I mock the red-tailed hawk—
His battle-bird's cry. The vulture's croak
And, so too, the lovely mew of the curlew
Roll trippingly, grippingly off my tongue
As I sit here sauced gabbing like a huckster
Or a gombeen man. Pie completes my name;
Maggot begins it and eats the end.

Who am I?

—AFTER RIDDLE 24, *Exeter Book*

Alexander Wilson's Essential Magpie

Magpie: a bird destructive to orchards and gardens,
Noisy and restless, flitting always from place to place;
So fond of carrion is this corvid, he alights on bovines'
Backs to feast on larvae festering in the shoulder flesh.
But the bird eats all sorts of vegetables as well as fruits.
He sups greedily on grains, worms, and divers insects.
When domesticated, magpie learns and imitates
The human voice, articulating words most distinctly.
Dishonorably he displays his tribe's pilfering habits,
Filling every chink, nook, and empty dim-lit space
With whatever offal he can thieve and hoard away.
So halting's his gait, he surely suffers epileptic fits.
    Measure by measure, this fowl's essentially absurd,
    Decidedly rotten, the most unbecoming of birds.

Snag Breac at Glendalough, Co. Wicklow

> On Christmas night in the year 835 the pagan Vikings
> raided two of the great monasteries of Ireland: St. Kevin's at
> Glendalough & the Clonmore monastery of St. Mogue.
>
> —IRISH ANNALS

1

Walk wind-wracked shores by two lakes within
The glen. Ascend the raked and narrow path,
Rise to St. Kevin's church. Then wind round
The tower, stand beneath the plinth of lichened
Stone. Hold still. Wait and watch the clouds
Scarf granite slopes while winter flaws bitter
As sin white-cap the waters that brim the glen.
Breathe, draw in the silent solstice damp and wind.

2

First upon the narrow path, you appear *ex nihilo*,
You thieving bird, so self-assured and loud
Your song can't be missed (bleating like a lamb,
Shrieking like a shrike), but then you lift, flashing
Wings of iridescent green and blue on black,
And fly to light among the tilting tombstones,
A spot forever sorrow-swept and swooned
When berserkers felled screaming, fleeing monks,
Hacked their limbs and rolled their holy heads
Upon a goat-groomed lawn by the burning oratory.

3

Up the plinth you rise to grate against the grain
As if to spite the pull of gravity. So I wait
And watch you prove there is no fear in love.
Hopping, rising up, you wind a gyre of your own
Round Kevin's tower, talons taut on hand-
Hewn stone, gripped sure against the gale.
And the half-true rhyme of your timeless tune

Recalls an ancient lay, a monkish dream of
Hope sung in shades of black and white:

> *Black is the bitter wind tonight*
> *It tousles the ocean's white mane*
> *So we fear not berserkers*
> *Coursing the Irish Sea.*

Magpie Rises Coming Down to Earth

Where the body is, there too shall be the magpie.
—SOME GOSPEL OF JESUS (TRANSLATION MINE)

The magpie is not a true creature of the sky . . .
The magpie is more a creature of the ground or trees.
—FRED RYSER, *Birds of the Great Basin*

1

On black extended wings magpie scans
And scouts the fallen world with dark devouring
Eyes from heights pressed still and flat against the sun—
So he tracks, then targets plain and simple pickings.

Before he lights though magpie makes a rainbow show,
A kind of wavelength flight on blue black wings—
A coaster ride that in the solstice sun hues iridescent
Green, a rising rush below the sheltering sky, a curving
Climb by which he nearly clips a twist of scrub oak crowns,
Then falls and dips and lofts again before his sortie ends,
Touching softly down in meadow grass lush and tall.

Looking, listening, ear cocked to the ground,
Magpie scries for secret signs of tiny maggot flies
Or beetle grubs whose work it is to feast,
To thrive on all that's left behind to ripe and rot
And thus help this our spent and weary earth revive.

2

Above the snowbound mountain
In a cloudless cobalt sky
It seemed the only moving thing
Was a jet-black Magpie eye.
Then all went still when within
His retina scan, a streak of red
On white, a strip of scarlet flesh,
Into the corvid's focus came,

And in that vision same
A jigsaw spine of black-on-white,
A heartbeat line that puzzled fine
Through a slain songbird's skull—
A bone-ball crimsoned from the kill,
Also there, beside the songbird's head,
An ouroboros forsaken & forgotten,
A snake of grey and purpled innards coiled
Round a gizzard bulged by death & grainy sand—
    So Magpie lit and feasted.

The Bird Refused

for Seamus Heaney

She lay dead felled by bird shot.
No sober thought of desecration ever
crossed his tender mind when he pinched
and quickly tugged to pluck the feathers
from the songbird's sorry sagging skull.
Her head was bare and white now, freckled
slightly red so that the sight appalled him,
This hapless, balded bird recalled his mother
without her woolen cap on the cancer ward.
To salve the wound he laughed and chanted:
Sing professor, sing, that's truly what he said
while he plucked a jig-saw path of down
to show a shattered windpipe, pink and raw.
Then the boy, he blew but nothing, *nada, nichts*
went out or in or through the haggised
battered thrapple. The broken bird
stayed silent still refused his breath,
refused to sing again.

On Seeing a Jakhodo Scroll Painting Entitled *Magpie (Village Spirit) & Tiger (Mountain Spirit)*

A tiger in the forest stumbles in the mire.
He can't free himself. He waits, watches.
Three days stuck without food he suffers
Before a woodcutter hears desperate
Caterwauling from the slop and muck.

Tiger begs woodcutter to spare his life.
When the man obliges, tiger rudely tries
To eat him. Distressed, the woodcutter
Begs an ox and pine tree to settle his fate,
But the jury's split: ox says tiger must eat;
The crooked tree says, *Set the poor soul free.*

Distraught, woodcutter implores a magpie
Perched in the jachelt pine. Magpie orders
Woodcutter and tiger to reenact the story
So he can see who is the cleverer of the two.
Idiot tiger enters mud. Magpie saves the man.

—AFTER A KOREAN FOLK TALE AND FOLK PAINTING

The beauty of the world is the mouth of a labyrinth. The unwary individual who on entering takes a few steps is soon unable to find the opening. Worn out, with nothing to eat or drink, in the dark, separated from his dear ones, and from everything he loves and is accustomed to, he walks on without knowing anything or hoping anything, incapable even of discovering whether he is really going forward or merely turning round on the same spot. But this affliction is as nothing compared with the danger threatening him. For if he does not lose courage, if he goes on walking, it is absolutely certain that he will finally arrive at the center of the labyrinth. And there God is waiting to eat him. Later he will go out again, but he will be changed, he will have become different, after being eaten and digested by God. Afterward he will stay near the entrance so that he can gently push all those who come near into the opening.

—SIMONE WEIL, *Waiting for God*

Feeder off Battlefields

1

Magpie spies killing fields spread all before him—
With a heart joyous nor scared by its own rapacity,
He looks about and, below a bank of clouds
Bedizening orange and daffodilly skies, the bird he sees
A world not changed since the first blood-dimmed tide
Came roiling in, that morning when, somewhere East
Of Eden, Cain conked Abel, the day that wombed
The never-healing wound, a wound unbound,
Rubbed forever raw and round by brothers killing brothers,
Unworlding wounds of battlegrounds filled by mounds
               On mounds of tombs—

2

On abandoned bison-roads that cleave the precious line
Between ripe and rot he roams. In troughs of feed
Which others might find awful and repulsive,
So breeds and multiplies the mystery of this bird,
This fowl so strange, a corvid curious and carnivorous,
Who loves whatever's weird (the worst of dregs and dirges
Dark yet somehow beautiful, of strange things heard
And only seen by those who know the art of laying low,
Ears cocked to the ground, bodies bowed reverently
Before pretty birds deceased and munching maggots),
A bird who seldom slaughters for a living,
Feeds and feasts off battlefields, butchering songs
Of life and death, strains ever ancient, ever new,
Unheimlich sights & sounds about what's hidden out of sight.

3

       Upon the tombed and broken ground
         Magpie stooped—and listening
           This is what he heard:

dig, dig, dig

So that is what he did.

A voice that was a wound came
Welling from the broken ground
Whispering like the sound
Of leaves rattling in an aspen;

    you feel trapped,
    dream escapes—
    but beware mirages;

    run not nor fly
    like blackbird who
    longs to be free;

    dig in the secret
    elderberry place
    given unto you:

    there find God
    despite darkness,
    spring and all—

    He floats not
    beyond horizons;
    God burrows in

    your (de)basement;
    pride runs always
    but **Love** digs;

    flee your solitude
    & your prison runs
    with you only

to collapse in the
slipstream of its
ravenous flight;

dig down too
so you will dis-
appear in Dieu.

4

Hearing songs from underground
songs of friends from forgotten wars
now he listened at a slab
of lakeside rock, a plinth of tilted granite,
     for the bird had heard vatic voices speak
through bones and trees and shore stones:

Sometimes the meridian sun
blood orange, darting like flames
flaring just beyond the ridge

sometimes fistfuls

of light

rain

or the strand littered with limbs,
strewn with shards of ancient glowing jars—

Put out the light, then put out the light.

Oh, friends from other wars, long silenced,
standing on this lonesome, cloudy shore,
   we remember you as day dusks—
you and all those beaten into the clay.

Everywhere the columns ruined, children killed,
   villages razed, millions on the move,
      broken walls and burning towers—

only the chapel on the hill
    holds still;
  it manifests—dark, sunken—
the power of the imperium against
    the silhouetted mountain at twilight.

Was it for this clay grew tall?

Then we heard footfall on shore stones.
The bird, though, he saw no faces;
    they'd gone before us.

But voices could be heard—
  though they'd grown gravid,
languid as when the ox is on the tongue,
    hanging in the heaven's veins,
    heavy beside the steady

      klick-klack
      klick-klack

of wave-wracked, cobbled shore stones:

Young bodies, loved and loving, have been here:
throbbing chests, salmon-colored shells,
    feet skimming the water undaunted

Was it for this clay grew tall?

  …Wheat ripens rapidly;
  it takes but a moment
  for the leaven of bitterness to rise,
  it doesn't take much time
  for evil to lift its head
  …there is an island.

    Piteous!
  Under the warrior's helmet
    weed-hopper wails.

In the dust of old ghost-roads, emptied bison-roads:

Odours that rise / When the spade wounds the roots of tree…

> *We all had on us the stench*
> *Of dead bodies. The bread*
> *We ate, the stagnant water,*
> *Everything we touched reeked*
> *Because the earth around us*
> *Was stuffed with corpses.*

It should break your heart to kill.

Voices of prophets / of poets upon the water

Where we lay down and wept

Voice of the Lord, *Kyrie eleison*

Here on this pebbled shore,
> *between the burial mounds, amnesia's best;*
> *Who can make her voice heard?*
> *Must each dream alone—never hearing*
> *the other's nightmare?*

Voice of the Lord upon the waters

The end of art is peace.

There is a place called *querencia*

> a garden place of peace.

A Ripe Rude Garden

The nineteenth-century Great Plains was a slaughterhouse. In the years from the 1820s to the 1920s, this single American region experienced the largest wholesale destruction of animal life discoverable in modern history.

—DAN FLORES, *American Serengeti*

Sent out Bratten and Frazier to kill the barking Squirel. / Gave directions to all to kill the Magpye / should they See any of the cunning birds. / we precured two of the barking Squirels only. / we are deturmined to delay one day / for purposes of collecting scelletins / of the Mule deer & antilope & more barking Squirels. / Several of the men with the Wives of the enterpreter / Jessomme & the Mandan Chief found plumb bushes / near the river bottom, gathering more fruit than the party / Could eat in two days; those plump plumbs being of three Speces, / the most of them large, well flavored. / This good place recalls the spot called Pleasant Camp, / from the great abundance of its ripe rude garden— / bounteous Game Such as Buffalow, Elk, antilopes, Blacktail or mule deer, / fallow deer, common deer, wolves, barking Squirels, / Turkies and various other animals, / added to which was a glorious abundance / of the most delicious plumbs & grapes. / And the hunters informed me / they Saw great numbers of Buffalow in the plains. / I Saw Several herds of those animals / on either Side today at a distance. / the river banks and beyond were crouded with buffaloe / I sincerely belief there were not / less than 10 thousand buffaloe within a circle / of 2 miles around that place.

—AFTER LEWIS AND CLARK'S JOURNALS, 1804–1806

Three Ways of Looking at Magpie— a Most Becoming Bird

You did not kill the fish only to keep alive and to sell for food, he thought. You killed for pride and because you are a fisherman. You loved him when he was alive and you loved him after. If you love him, it is not a sin to kill him. Or is it more?

—ERNEST HEMINGWAY, *The Old Man and the Sea*

Dried all our wet articles this fine Day, / Capt Lewis out with a View to see the Countrey / and its productions, gone all day; / killed a Buffalow and a remarkable Bird / of the *Corvus* Species, Magpy. / a butifull thing, this magpy.

—AFTER WM. CLARK'S ENTRY DATED 17 SEPT, 1804

one of the hunters killed a bird
of the *Corvus genus* and order of the pica
about the size of a jack-daw   with a tale remarkably long,
                        beautifully variegated.
these birds seldom appear in parties of more than three or four;
   most usually at this season, they range single as the halks (ravens)
        and other birds of prey commonly do—
from its sleak appearance I believe too
                      its usual food is flesh—
Pica hudsonia has an agreeable note
   something like a goald winged Blackbird,
      a note not disagreeable, though loud—
          twait twait twait, twait, twait, twait twait, twait.
Flying, this bird does not spread its tail
   & aloft its wing motions recall the Jay-bird's—

(its flying note— *tah, tah, tah, tah tah, tah, tah, tah*)
and the wings have nineteen feathers,
    forming a darkly colored triangle when spread—
dark but not jet or shining black; darker yet is the wing's underside.
The upper side of the wing is a dark blackish or bluish green
    sometimes tinting soft bluish or light orange yellow
in different light exposures—a kaleidoscope of color.

The plumage of the tale figures twelve feathers of equal lengths by pairs;
here, too, the feather bottom changes, refracting different portions of light:
    towards their extremity, these feathers hue orange-green,
    then, shaded, pass to a reddish indigo blue,
    and at their extremity assume the green of mutability—
the tinges of these beautiful feathers are not unlike
    but equally rich as the peacock's tints of blue and green—
    Magpie is a most becoming bird.

—AFTER MERIWETHER LEWIS'S ENTRY DATED 17 SEPT, 1804

Meriwether's measure of a magpie:

	Ft	In
from tip to tip of wing	1	10
Do. beak to extremity of tale	1	8 ½
of which the tale occupys		11
from extremity of middle toe to hip		5 ½

Hunger

In the deepest beatings of his hard old magpie heart
This common bird feels great shame at leaving anything
    Unused, unsavored, unsung—
      So he sings (or rather *yaks* and *maags*):

Nothing should ever be discarded, nothing dumped for naught,
And nevermore should ripeness be left on Lethe's shore to rot.

Like A Common Thief: Magpie Caught, Caged, Catalogued

—AFTER WM. CLARK'S JOURNAL: HIDATSA MANDAN VILLAGE,
APRIL THE 3RD, THURSDAY, 1805

    we Shall pack up to day
    and Set out tomorrow
    for the vast unknown—
    a white frost this morning,
    as bright as a magpie belly;
    some ice on the edge
    of the bank below which
    the water pools as black
    as that queer bird's crest.

observed equal altitudes of the ☉
                with Sextant and artificial horizon

Chronometer too fast 32 minets
observed Time and Distance of ☉ & ☽s
        nearest limbs withe Sextant and Chromometer—   Sun west

    a fine day to
pack up & prepare to load
    Sundery articles to be Sent
    to the President of the U. S.—

Box No. 1, contains the following articles i e'

Package No. 7 & 9. Horns of Black tailed deer, a Mandan bow & quiver of arrows—w/tobacco seed.

Package No. 12. The bones & Skeleton of a Small burrowing wolf of the praries.

Package No. 99 Box No. 2. Contains 4 Buffalow *Robes*, and an ear of Mandan Corn.

a Carrote of Ricaras *Tobacco and* a red fox Skin Containing a Magpie.

Package No. 15. Mandan *robe* containing 2 burrowing Squirels, a white *weasel* & Skin of a Loucirvea.

1 Robe representing a battle between the Sioux & Ricaras.

Cages No. 6 & No. 7. Contain a liveing burrowing Squirel of the prairies and 4 liveing magpies.

Ordway's journal, Wednesday, 3rd April 1805 (clear and pleasant)

> The articles which was to be Sent back
> to the States in the Big Barge was packed
> and boxed up ready to go on board.
>
> *To which entry, the Magpie requests a favor of reply:*
> *Of the live animals caged & shipped,*
> *only the prairie dog and one of the four magpies*
> *reached Mr. Jefferson alive—*
>   *an ill omen forsooth.*

In turn President Jefferson sent Charles Willson Peale the marmot & the surviving magpie for his museum of curiosities in Philadelphia.

Every Bone Must Find Its Fellow Bone: a Letter from C.W. Peale to Thomas Jefferson

12 January, 1806

Dear Mr. Jefferson,

The Skeletons are so much broken I fear the bones
Lost at places where crates were opened.
I can mend broken bones but cannot make good
The deficiency of lost ones, so them being mixed
Together is no great matter, but bones broken
Or lost hinder the progress of my museum—
For every bone must find its fellow bone.
Whether I can get an intire Skeleton from this mass
Of fragments, I cannot yet determine;
It will be a work of time, the exercise of much patience
Which I shall not lament, provided the object is accomplished
& the loss of bones proves my only obstacle in the work
Of restoring to them a semblance of their former life.

While the Marmot sleeps, the Magpye chatters in good health.
Now alive in the Museum, many creatures most interesting:
The Crown bird (*l'oiseau royal*), a Crowned Pidgion, Carrier
Pidgions, Western Buzzards, a Ringtail Macoco, and a Syrin
Or Mud-Iguana of a large size from Georgia, &c.
Diverse other creatures have I preserved in vigorous baptisms
Of water and arsenic. I am much obliged to Capt. Lewis
For increasing our knowledge of the territorial Animals.
I wish I could get one of the sheep with large horns
Such as those you have done me the favor of sending.
I shall primarily populate this Museum with American Beasts
Rather than those of other countryes, yet for a comparative view
This shop of curiosities shall show specimens from round the Globe!

Since the Philosophical Society owns an Elephant Skeleton,
I hope to give the Public a comparative view of the Pachyderm
Beside the Mammoth I have restored to roundness of form.

Mr. President, I want you much to see these Skeletons together.

Accept my best wishes for your health &c,

Charles Willson Peale

C.W. Peale's Recipe for Preserving Birds, &c,

Decay of the dead is best delayed
By vigorous baptisms of water and arsenic.
Then skin large birds (magpies, crows, &c)
In the following wise:
Scalpel with sharp knife from vent to breast,
Separating skin on each side
Until the thighs can be drawn through the skin,
Then sever the specimen at the leg joints.
Repeat same motion with wings to the pinion,
And in the pinion part of each wing draw
Out all possible flesh with the hooked wire.
Next, through the skin stretch the neck
Until you can cut it off near the skull;
This motion severs head from body and tail.
Having thus the skin separated from the body,
Use hook and brain spoon, evacuating brains entire
Through the rear of skull where neck was sliced.
With bone saw, cut out roof of mouth with care
And extract eyes from inside mouth by measures
and movements of extraction hook. Be delicate.

All manner of beasts may be skinned
By opening the belly, drawing the legs, and sawing
At the feet joints. With smallest, most fragile specimens,
The whole skin may be left, then treated with arsenic potion.
For the larger beasts, it shall suffice to cut off from the head
Such part as will reveal the upper and under teeth,
Which remain attached to the skin—

Slather salt on skins of beasts,
                                          but never on the birds.

Zebulon Pike Marvels at Magpies Scavenging in the Snow Shadow of Mt. Shavano

The difficulty of procuring food being general and widespread in these circumstances rendered the magpies so bold as to light on our men's arms and eat from their hands.

—ZEBULON PIKE

>The storm continuing with violence,
>We remained encamped above the river.
>One of our hunters out but killed nothing.
>
>The snow by night one foot deep.
>Our horses obliged to scrape drifts
>Away with hooves and tongues
>To obtain a miserable pittance
>Of brittle, withered fescues.
>
>To increase the beasts' misfortunes,
>Magpies attack the wretched equines.
>Lured by putrescent, oozing wounds
>Atop the horses' backs, the birds alight
>On the miserable creatures, and in defiance
>Of the horses' neighing, wincing, kicks,
>They prick them further raw and pick.

—AFTER *The Southwestern Journals of Zebulon Pike*, 1ST OF DEC, 1806

The Raising of the Dead

Bluebird married Elk Woman first, then Buffalo Woman. Bluebird favored the first bride, mistreated the second. So Buffalo Woman ran away with her son, Calf Stands Up, to the home of the buffalo people. Bluebird pursued his wife to the land of the buffalo people and there he saw the buffalo dance. Bluebird demanded his wife return to his home, but before he was allowed to leave with his family, Buffalo Chief proclaimed Bluebird would have to pass many tests, which included selecting his son from a group of calves that looked exactly like Calf Stands Up and running a race against young bulls. There was a final test, too, which was the hardest. And so Calf Stands Up was able to help his father in every test but the last. For his final test, Bluebird would have to stay awake through four nights and four days of storytelling. Calf Stands Up couldn't take his father's place in the sleep ordeal. Bluebird's head began to nod as the second night of storytelling ended. At last, Bluebird's eyes grew so heavy he sank into a deep sleep as the sun began to rise on the third day. When the sun passed the horizon, the buffalo began to dance. Round and round they churned, trampling the body of the man until he was ground into the earth. Now before he had set out on his journey, Bluebird had told his brother, Magpie, that if harm came to him among the buffalo, a plume of dust would rise to the heavens. Indeed, as the buffalo danced over his body, a dust-devil gyred upwards. And so Magpie told Elk Woman, *What my brother told me has come to pass. Make a sweat-lodge and I will search for a piece of his body.* Magpie entered the dust cloud and soon he heard groaning nearby. He followed the wounded sound and found a feather which Bluebird had worn on his head. Gripping the feather in his beak, Magpie flew back home and carried the feather into the sweat-lodge. After placing it there, he went out and stood at the south-east corner and prayed, *Father, I have brought back my brother.* As he said this, he shot a black arrow straight into the sky and hollered, *Watch out brother or the arrow will strike you.* In the same way, he shot another black arrow from the southwestern corner, then red arrows from each of the two remaining corners. Each time he squawked his warning, the lodge quaked from within. At the fourth warning, when he shouted, *Watch out brother the arrow will strike you*, the osier frame shook more violently yet, and his brother appeared, standing in the middle of the lodge. Bluebird said, *I have much to tell you, but first we must prepare for the arrival of the buffalo. They are coming back and will be angry.*

—AFTER EDWARD CURTIS'S APPROPRIATED VERSION
OF AN ARAPAHO MYTH

Everything is changed but nothing perishes. The spirit wanders, going hence, thither, coming thence, hither and takes possession of any limbs it pleases. With equal ease it goes from beasts into human bodies and from us into beasts, nor in any length of time does it fail. And as wax is easily molded into new shapes, nor remains as it had been before, nor keeps the same form, but yet is itself the same, so do I teach that the soul is ever the same, but migrates into different shapes.

—OVID, *Metamorphoses*, 15:165–176

My intention is to tell of bodies changed into new forms.

—OVID, *Metamorphoses*, 1:1

Becoming Magpie

*Let mind be changed from a man's and let a beast's mind
be given to him: and let seven periods of time pass over him.*

—DANIEL 4:16

1

A magpie lit on a songbird nest in a pine outside my window.
That fowl wasn't Levine's or Miłosz's magpie, or some old drunk
Monk's magpie, or a beatnik bird in Gary Snyder's song.
No, that bird was genuine, truer than my shadow self and I—
Not some wannabe like me, falling always short of magpiety.

2

There was a bird—not just any bird—all decked in black
And white, a barely fledged and freakish sight, the yin and yang
I'd longed for, and though he sometimes struggled with his song
Still he cawed and crooned full throated, lonely, sad beneath
The planets, stars and crimson moon, chanting timeless tunes
Of beasts and birds and men alike transformed into each other.

3

The bird he spoke no word
But looked upon the window glass
Like seeing darkly through a mirror
And seemed to tilt his head and smile.

4

Seeing him,
Somehow the man I am
Began to molt and shed his skin,
Shifted shape becoming something strange and new,
A force focused on the here-and-now,
A bird-man more becoming than before,
Who sprouted down of white below his breast,

Formed freedom wings with rainbowed feathers
Of iridescent green and blue—
So man and magpie merged and grew.

Now we're corvids two, brothers of a feather
Singing together from the rims of songbird nests,
Where we strike up songs of absent mama wrens
And warblers. They're haunting melodies,
Yet sweeter still unheard by baby birds,
For we're said to gouge the eyes of unsuspecting
Chicks and eat them whole before we rise and fall
To pillage nests of other threatened songbirds.

5

We magpies, too, are wont to make a decent
Living not by dint of mayhem, malice, slaughter,
But by licking, tasting, chewing scraps fallen
And forgotten off a gourmand's plate, the sort
Of slop pampered prigs loathe and hate.

Mounds and mounds of lovely offal,
                    Magpies eat it all—

On icy winter days, the maggot worm
Or beetle grub we might forego and
Choose instead to craft a *koan*,
That speaks of making strange, while
Feasting from a greasy dumpster.

So we thrive, drinking of the dregs,
Savoring everything shunned and left
To fester, ripe, and rot by others.
Thus runs the road less trod, a path
Between the crooked post and gate
Whereon we listen, watch, and wait
Before we chart our way to magpiety.

Haggis

With wife and kids away, he cleared a space for dalliance. He scooped a tablespoon full of everything on the counter—mashed potatoes, peas and turnips, kielbasa. He stuffed it all into his gob. This was his little secret, performed in solitude. He chewed, rolled it all up into one ball, then spat it on the plate. *Thud.* He repeated the process, launching another ball. *Thud.* It was nothing like that familiar hollow morning sound, the metallic ring of children pouring cereal into breakfast bowls. *Thud.* Sound of substance. He admired the way the orbs looked. Like *haggis*. *Haggis*—strange word. So foreign and familiar. Three times he said the weird word: *Haggis, haggis, haggis.* Ah, from *l'agace*, of course, he mused. *L'agace*: old French, some sort of bird word, he recalled. Mouthing the word slowly, he stressed each syllable. Making strange was in his larynx, in his bones. He liked the sensation generated by the word vibrating off his tongue, thrumming under the roof of his mouth. Mouth music. The sound pleased him. He longed now to see the word spelled out. Into his phone, then, he typed *l'agace*. Letter by letter the word materialized. Miraculous: through an intragalactic tap, one could uncover a bird word, dig deep into its fossil record. *L'agace*: perhaps from *hachheiz*, Old French for *minced meat*, which gave way to *l'agace*, ancient French for "magpie." Analog of the odds and ends collected by the bird or perhaps a nod to the fowl's appetite for raw flesh. He felt more hunger rumble, gurgle in his gut. He bit and chewed again, but now sans fork. He ate directly by the beak. He chewed, minced the mélange, rolled it up into one ball, then watched it drop and fall upon his plate. *Hachheiz*, he said. Sounds Germanic. He much preferred saying, hearing the lovely, tender French— *l'agace*. How smoothly it lilted off the tongue; he spoke the word again, slowly, lovingly, mouthing each vowel gradient, feeling letter by strange letter, the sweet tension of each syllable's soft explosion within his gob. *L'agace, l'agace, l'agace* is what he said before slipping into a whispered *magpie, magpie, magpie.*

Gertrude Stein on a Soul's Miraculous Migration to Magpiety

I saw [in photographs] how St. Thérèse existed from the life of an ordinary young lady to that of the nun. So everything was actual, and I went on writing.

—GERTRUDE STEIN

On the Boulevard Raspail
There floats a place on watery air
Where they fashion photographs,

Pictures that I've always loved.
There they make image after
Image of a young girl dressed

In the costume of ordinary life
And little by little, slowly
In a photographic river-run

She transforms into a nun:
A saint, uncomplicated, selfless,
Dressed in black and white,

Light and darkness indivisible—
A *memento mori* of forty still lifes
For friends and family when

The girl is dead, *in memoriam*.

Holding Still, Becoming Magpie

In Gertrude's landscapes nothing really moves
But things are there like magpies in the air
Over the fields of Ávila or Lisieux—holding

Still—the birds lie flat upon the sky,
As in Annunciation scenes where the Holy Spirit rests,
Pressed high and level against the heavens.

None of which is possible in actuality. Birds can't hold still
In flight, to hang suspended in a blue and cloudless sky.
Yet Saints do say, *With God everything's possible, all shall be well.*

So's the suggestion in the grainy image train: a girl is first
A longhaired lass, then frame by frame she becomes
A shorn nun, an icon of magpiety in black and white.

What's more bold and beautiful than a shorn, silent nun—
A bird of black & white, holding still, pressed flat against the sun?

The Girl in the Village

One day in the mist shrouded hills of the Sierra Madre Occidental, an unfortunate *niña* returned home from school and wafted into the family hovel on the dark wings of a foul odor, a death stench that clung to her like flies on carrion. Each day the whiff of putrefaction tightened its noose. Soon the girl's father removed his daughter's bed to the meager courtyard garden where the family goat and dog slept. In the corner of the courtyard a caged magpie clung shivering to his cactus perch. For two years, the bird had refused to sing, refused to speak. This was so since the girl's father bartered for the talking magpie in a trade made with a Basque shepherd. That was up in Idaho, in the sheep pastures, before the bird went mute, before the father brought the magpie home. The odor persisted so the father, desperate, turned to the local dentist for assistance. A gringo ex-pat, the dentist was a hack who doubled as a barber. Initially, he filed down the girl's molars and incisors, but this remedy failed. So he extracted all her teeth on the hunch that the stench stemmed from rotting roots beneath the gums. This fix fell short as well. Shortly thereafter the village priest pronounced a fast to drive out the demons behind the mischief. The mayor considered playing his part by lowering the national colors to half-staff and cancelling the poor girl's *quinceañera*. But all such measures were for naught. The reek of fetid flesh continued to permeate the family courtyard. Then one spring morning, as butterflies and the song of mockingbirds returned to the highlands, the local pine forest belched a cloud of yellow pollen. When she awoke that day, the girl sneezed ferociously. As she blew and fingered her nose hunting for a booger, her nail snagged a thick, half-decomposed rubber band. The mayor declared a holiday and the girl's father freed the magpie. A small leftist paper in Patzcuaro picked up the story and reported that the girl had apparently stuffed the rubber band up her nose as a toddler. As she grew into puberty and her mucus production increased, the foreign object began to rot. So ran the story. Such a thing has happened.

The Conejos County Magpie program that started May 1 resulted in a total of $885 paid in bounties so far. Sanford community leads the contest with a total of 11,180 eggs and 2,722 heads taken. This represents a sum of $359.70 in bounties.

—The Steamboat Springs Pilot,
THURSDAY, JUNE 21, 1951

A Prayer for T.H., My Magpie, & Me

A sense of sin: the one indispensable quality of a novelist.
—FRANÇOIS MAURIAC

Raymond Chandler is gazing out
The bay window of a beachside rancher.
The sky, cloudless, mirrors the brilliant blue
And broad expanse of the Pacific south of Malibu.

He turns his eye from sea and sky to his wife who's
Reading Stevens' "Sunday Morning" in an old cane
Rocker. Monotone, he says, *I don't like the view—*
Too much ocean. Too many drowned men. Too many dead birds.

Lord, spare Ted, the bird, and me—
Spare us a sense of doom.
Spare us most of the dark side, too,
But grant us, Lord, sense enough of sin
So we don't drown when the blood-
Brimmed tide comes roiling in.

Ubi Sunt

We played the pipe for you, and you did not dance;
we sang a dirge, and you did not mourn.

—MATTHEW 11:17

I hunker in a forest boltered by my brother's blood.
I'm a magpie on the margin and own but a paltry heap
Of pilfered goods—a dried newt, a tattered braid of yarn,
A shekel tarnished, four chokecherry pits, a brush once
Owned by Farrah Fawcett, a shot glass brimmed with DDT.
My dwelling is a keep commandeered from a restless linnet.
My middle kingdom is the spirit's *buan*, a desolate dominion
Shunned even by the sun. My bed's a bowl of twigs
Lined with mud and finest rootlets. My loose roof's a dome
Of sticks and trinkets speckled by star shine, moonlight.
Sometimes I flee to a waste of wilderness at mountain's edge.
Perched on the ledge between hell and heaven, a spot near
The cliff where the Angel of Light tempted the Teacher,
I look about and stare with a heart sorrowed and scared.
The whole world lies before me and should the guide
I choose be nothing better than a chemical cloud,
I cannot lose my way, for we find the massacre
No matter where we wander, desecration lies all about.

    Where are all the forest trees?
                Where the toads and crickets?
Where are all the honey bees?
                Where the rider and the horse?
Where is the horn that was blowing?
                Where the slender-billed grackle
And passenger pigeon, the least
                vermillion flycatcher and kakawie,
The Carolina parakeet, the bush wren
                and the highland capercaillie?

Where, oh where, are the snows of yesteryear?
                Where's the remorse for all this destruction?

Rites of Passage at the Feast of Lupercal, 1973

> *When you have shot one bird flying you have shot all birds flying. They are all different and they fly in different ways but the sensation is the same and the last one is as good as the first.*
>
> —ERNEST HEMINGWAY, "Fathers and Sons"

Between the curling sweet pea tendrils, through the budding almond trees, I saw them pounding, schwacking heads and throats and wings as in a slumber party pillow war. Crack, crack, spat the shotguns. Poof, blew the targets like the burst of pillow sacks or hemorrhaged hearts. Through the fence, I watched them cool their guns, heard them screech, *It's raining feathers, raining feathers.* That is what they said. But feathers neither fall nor drop like rain. Feathers float like snowflake flurries, silent at the witching hour of a winter's night; and feathers drift like downy cherry blossom showers at the start of spring. There was no rain or snow, though, on that bone-cold day. Just a drift of feathers amid the falling almond blossoms, and birds were dropping dead. And earth was damp with tears and blood. Rosied carpets spread across the waking earth. Ring around the rosie...and roses are red. Feathers are blue—and white and black, and iridescent green. God is Love...and all fall down. And crimson's the blood of the spilled cup that blooms and pinks the snow. So as I was saying, my friends turned fiends. I see their devil's dance, see it still. They're prancing, chanting: *It's raining feathers.* There I am. Hands hanging at my sides. Dumb fuck butcher boys, children of the fox and wolf, *luperci*, out shooting poor man's skeet. Potting magpies.

> the nuns in black and white,
> told the boys who loved both God and guns
> *Sweet Lord of Mercy, Love Divine*
> *Let that be your Valentine*

Why a killing spree on the feast of Valentine, a massacre fit for rites of Lupercal? My friends turned cruel that day and found my secret magpie place around the granite monoliths and oaks. Beastie boys, they hoofed and rent the wet green earth, clawed raw the sacred ground till blood ran riot. Drip drop. Get your swollen adolescent rocks off killing birds. As I watched and waited, I blinked and tried to think it through, but couldn't cry. *It's raining feathers?* Right as rain, now it's pouring rain. Red rain, redrum. Seven magpie bodies fell to Earth that day. *What goes up must come down*, is also what they sang. Battered, shattered birds filth the sacred oak grove's grassy plain. But then as now, no room for argument. Talking, words, words and talking—they've never stayed the slaughter. What I said was nothing. What I say is nothing. The ox is on the tongue. Struck dumb, my tongue hangs limp, thick and still like tule fog. No way to stop the rain. No way to shore the bare and ruined choirs where late the sweet birds sang. The hunter's bag bears witness. Five decades hence, bodies just keep raining down. For no good reason, no reason that the stones or bones or trees can tell—no reason but for gravity, for lack of grace. On this rent and weary Earth, no mercy now or ever, always everywhere just gravity. Gravid is the word. All obey its law. Body of boar and bison, bird and lamb—and even man. Shoot them, knock them off a cliff or limb. See, it's so much fun. *It's raining feathers*. A body is a body is a body. Acceleration's all the same—32 feet per second per second—the same as rain. It falls and falls and falls—no matter what the season, spring or autumn, no matter what the day or celebration: July the Fourth, the feast of Tet, or the rites of Lupercal. *Rain, rain go away*—no, it just keeps raining. Feathers. Feathers. Feathers.

Grief Observed

*Blessed are they that mourn.
They shall be comforted.*
—ANOTHER GOSPEL OF JESUS

When they'd killed the magpies
And the hooligans had cooled
Their guns and slouched away
That cold, cruel Valentine's Day,
I thought it was my lot to mourn
The dead, to tend the big-time
Wound left to rot in winter sun.

Alone I stood in that garden waste
When I had the thought I ought to dig
A grave to spare their bone-crates
From coyotes and the hungry hounds.

Then in a burst of brilliance, the sky
Brimmed with magpies, a flash of
Illumination—in black and white:
A host of magpie kith and kin come
Back to tend and keen the fallen.

Landing next the strewn corpses
They began a cawing ululation—
Pecking, prodding, preening the limp
And lifeless bodies dressed in red,
Iridescent blue, black and white.

Soon a few of that keening crew
Plucked and gleaned, off a nearby

Green, newly sprouted leaves of grass
Which they bore, then laid upon
The rent and blood-stained earth
Around their magpie brethren's heads—

Were these not corvid wreaths of grief?

Ghorbân*

a Poem of Sacrifice

    The curtain falls upon the ground;
    in Helmand lopes a hungry hound;
    a cocksure beast that's long of tooth,
he churns and chews this bloodied earth:

      we lie in stillness all around
    not far from others on this Earth—
     whatever once it was that bound
        us in our love lies cold
  and sheaved between our teeth—
   the curtain falls upon the ground.

—AFTER GERRIT ACHTERBERG'S *"Slagveld"* (1940)

*Ghorbân is Dari for "sacrifice"

Magpie Rues the Cherry Orchard

I used to love the orchard evenings,
Streams of light slant-shimmered
Between the trees and irrigation ditch
Upon the late day sward. The whiff
Of blackberry bramble, licorice, mint
Growing on the banks. When I was young
Grandfather liked to lead us to the ranch
To feed among the cherry trees. Kind
And mindful was the rancher. One day
He disappeared. A new man came who
Cursed us. On the spot he shot my dad,
My uncle in the face for stealing cherries—
Tossed them on the cider apple heap to rot.
Now the thought of that ranch makes me retch.

Perhaps One World...
but Please Not One Word for Bird

Language is fossil poetry.

—RALPH WALDO EMERSON

One language goes extinct about every two weeks, more frequently than bird extinction...Irish is expected to survive at least through this century, but half of the world's almost 7,000 remaining languages may disappear by 2100, experts say.

—FROM A MARCH 16, 2009 *WASHINGTON POST* STORY,
"Preserving Language Is About More Than Words"

When Magpie hatched out naked as a jay
8,000 languages adorned the Earth.
Babel had come to rule the roost, so it seemed.
But then the British bloke spoke on the BBC:
Unity is the basis of culture, he beamed.
And a joker in a white house jived, *E pluribus unum.*
So the vowel gradient of the Queen's English
And a Texas two-step twang covered the orb
Like a fog drifting through the Bosphorus
As pestiferous as white phosphorous
Choking throats, seeding the ague, and threatening
Tongues from Turkey to Peru, from Cairo to Timbuktu.

And with each passing day, the glib destroyers say,
Let us purify the dialect of every tribe.
So Magpie's world grows dumber with this severing,
This sloughing of the tongues, and the world grows
Smaller, more prosaic through the loss of language,
Moving closer, ever closer to one word—
One word for bird, but ever farther,
Ever further from the truth.

Riddle Second

When gone are all the songbirds
Singing from the trees
What in the world
Will the last bird-word be?

Answer: Magpie

Albanian	laraskë	Basque	mika	Belarusian	балбатун
Armenian	շաղակրատ	Bengali	বাচাল	Catalan	garsa
Chinese	鵲 (què)	Croatian	svraka	Czech	straka
Danish	husskade	Dutch	ekster	Estonian	harakas
Finnish	harakka	French	pie	**Cheyenne**	**moʼēʼha**
Georgian	კაჭკაჭი	German	Elster	Greek	καρακάξα
Hindi	अधेला	Irish	snag breac	Italian	gazza
Japanese	カサ	Khemer	ប៉ក្សី	Romanian	coțofană
Spanish	urraca	Ukrainian	сорока	Welsh	bioden

Annihilate Is an English Word

The bird unites in its character courage / and cunning, turbulency and rapacity. / Magpie is formed not inelegantly. / Distinguished by gay and splendid plumage, / Magpie's habits are familiar and despised / in those parts of the kingdom where he resides.

He is particularly pernicious to plantations / of young oaks, tearing up the acorns, / also to birds, destroying great numbers / of their eggs and young, even baby Chickens, / partridges, grouse, and pheasants. / On the last account, the vengeance Entire / of the game laws has been let loose lately / upon him in parts of England, Ireland, / Scotland, Wales where premiums are offered / for his head / and where this savage is / known by diverse names—*athaid, pioden, snag breac*— / but no matter how this bird be called, all agree /

                      he is as an arch and evil poacher—

Penalties are inflicted on those who permit / him to breed on their premises. Under the lash / of rigorous persecution, a few years / of measured patience will happily exterminate the tribe / annihilate the magpie entirely from the land.

—AFTER ALEXANDER WILSON'S *American Ornithology* (1808)

*Cheyenne Chief Mo'ē'ha (Magpie)
Refuses to Disappear As the White Man Wished*

Is it possible to live without feasting on death?
—WALKER PERCY, *Love in the Ruins*

A Scientist Marvels at Magpie Mob Tactics

> ...the idea that the success of human evolution, the way our species has come to dominate the earth, had to do fundamentally with our being social, being members of a pack.
>
> —ROBERT HAAS CHANNELING E.O. WILSON ON THE EVOLUTION OF HUMAN SOCIAL BEHAVIORS

Intent on witnessing interactions between magpies and members of the genus *elgaria*, a scientist released an alligator lizard into a large enclosure housing three captive magpies. The woman noted the reptile's defensive stance. High above the floor, the lizard arched its body toward the curious birds. Protecting his neck on the side from which the magpie mob stood ready to attack, the lizard tilted his head sideways, curved slightly downward. His cocked-and-ready jaw was completely ajar. The lizard bent the rest of his taut body just slightly. His tail trailed behind, forming a half circle. The largest magpie approached cautiously, then blitzed the lizard. The bird jackhammered the slender, scaly tail. A sudden tightening, then straightening of the lizard's body ensued before he sprang at his assailant. The magpie leapt rearward. Other members of the mob probed, tested their target. At each assault, the lizard appeared bemused, perhaps even bored. He calmly stood his ground. These operations continued for several minutes before each magpie retreated to a separate corner of the cage. Divided by a span of three meters from each bird, the lizard struggled to track the magpies' dispersed positions.

Redoubling their attacks, the magpies took rapid turns approaching the target, but the lizard charged straight ahead, bulling forward a foot or more to drive each bird away. Soon, these individual enfilades gave way to paired, then group assaults. Pressing their quarry from opposite directions, all three magpies suddenly grew excited, hopping round the lizard. The birds took turns darting in, delivering precision strikes upon the tail. The limitations of lizard vision prevented him from tracking more than one assailant at a time. Twisting himself into knots, the lizard failed to shift attention from one attacker to another quickly enough. He appeared to be suspended in slow motion, while the birds' movements shifted into warp speed. Blow upon blow struck the tail which the magpies were now managing to mince and sever. When the tail unhinged from the lizard's body at last, none of the birds tried touching it. Still, the lizard held his ground, showed no interest in escape. Now he launched his own offensive—chasing, gapping, lunging at the birds. But then, suddenly, the lizard shot to the nearest shelter, a dish in the cage. He hid there. The three birds stood mesmerized before the squirming tail. In time, one of the magpies overpowered and ate the tail. The birds made no further search for the reptile. In subsequent experiments, many other lizards were likewise placed in the magpies' cage. The scientist witnessed, with relish, each member of the *elgaria* genus displaying similar defense reactions against the force of magpie mob attacks.

Force, the Hero

Translate: probably from [L] *translat-us*, pa. pple. of *transferre* to TRANSFER. I.1. *trans*. To bear, convey, or remove from one person, place or condition to another; to transfer, transport; also *(obs)*, to remove the dead body or remains of a saint, or a hero or great [wo]man, from one place to another.

  Force the hero.
  Force, both subject and predicate
  at the heart of every sentence in *The Iliad*.
  Force of men and arms.
  Force forcing man—and woman.
  Force of no words—just deeds, brutal deeds:
  here the human body bends and breaks,
    and, as if by surge or swell,
     is swept away
    (oh, bitter salt-blinding wave),
  swept away by the force we all believed
    could be controlled
     (but now we lie
      deformed, deranged—
     struck dumb
   by that force of gravity
    to which we did succumb).

  Force defined: a faceless *x* which turns
    a body
     into a shattered bone-house.

  Exercised at its limits,
  Force severs soul and body.
  See Force making mockery of souls.
  Now you see souls, now you don't.
  Voila, corpses.
  A feast for magpies.

A show *The Iliad* never wearies of...
A show the world never wearies of...

And the poet sang:
...*horses rattled empty chariots through battle lines seeking their noble drivers.*
But on the ground they lie dearer to vultures and pies than to their wives.

Chariots drag once-human-heroes
    like rakes
        face down
           furrowing bloodied mud.

And the blind singer sang:
...*spread all around his black hair; in the soaked clay his whole head lies;*
once-lovely head; now Zeus lets demon-others defile it on this native soil.

See the spectacle undiluted.
Here no comforting artifice assuages.
In the dirt and muck there is no room
    for supreme fictions—
        of beauty, glory, nations, freedom, immortality.

No whited, vaterland-loving halo descends on this once-human head:

And the memory-keeper sang:
...*limbs pass to Hades, soul flees, laments its fate, forsakes its youth and vigor.*

Some things seem still more painful,
    poignant:
Now the Force of *The Iliad* cuts
to another world shattered
just as quickly;
a world far away, precious,
that necessary dream,
beneath the towers
that never-never-land of peace,

of the family,
that first world
where each soul should count more
than anything to those she loves.

His song rings out today:
*...ordering shining-haired palace maids to place the tripods on
the hearth, Andromache tells them to prepare Hector's after-battle bath.
What fondness. Oh, fond woman. Already, he lies cold far from hot baths,
slain by grey-eyed Athena, she who aimed Achilles' arms.*

Far from hot baths.
Hector's not alone.
The Iliad, most all of it,
occurs far from hot baths.
Hosts of souls, the great part
of the great host, both then and now,
live and perish in aching flesh
far from hot baths.

—AFTER HOMER AND SIMONE WEIL

Lizard Brain

In search of lizard-hunting fun
 our boyhood band of brothers
  would jettison the yellow bus
   and run full bore
into the winding esker field.

There we'd boulder up glacial scars
 scattered across the earth,
  among the ancient oaks—
granite shafts and cromlechs that eons
earlier had split, shattered, spread
  like a thousand urns and altars
strewn by a frigid river-run,
  the slow-measured churn
and frozen march of ancient ice-flows.

Straight up the polished mossy stone
we'd go, clutching, clawing as we climbed
  and just below the top
   in stealth we'd slow,
  then shimmy up the final yard
of tilted monolith to stop and perch
   upon the cool round summit
where moss gives way to lichened granite.

Playing a homespun sport called noosing,
   we stalked a path primeval that led to insight:
     through a game of wiles, with handmade noose
   we'd track, snag, tame, and thus set loose
both our & lizard's ancient wisdom of survival.

Wielding a pendant hang-man's knot
     wrought from string or floss—
but one as easily improvised
   from stalks of jimson weed strong and taut—
we'd wait & watch the cathedral rock
    scanning for our prey while
      holding still and wide-eyed
           as Carmelites in ecstasy.

There upon the promontory,
   out of stony fractures thin,
blue-bellies would suddenly appear
   and in a blur they'd scurry upward
then stop to sun themselves awhile
   or scout out unsuspecting prey.

   What we prized were males,
the sex that marks its hunting
   ground and attracts a mate
      with a sucking-in-of-sides
   and a head-tilt upwards
to expose a throat as blue as Tahoe
   on a hundred-mile January day.

When a bull would stop,

and stand his ground,
from behind we'd creep,
    like snakes surreptitious,
slithering sans sound in long green grass,
    or like a silent moccasin beside a seep—
  slow and slower and still unseen
    we'd spool out noose line
then reel it gently back until the finely
    angled, scaly diamond head
      breached the void
    between the hanging "O"
      and with a tug and jerk
    we'd cinch the knot.

Playing tender with our captured prey
fed a curiosity cruel and kind at once,
  for when we pinched the weirdly sticky
  ribs above the underbelly's velvet blue
    the creature was sure to crane
    and twist his un-noosed head,
then with his chiseled jaw he'd try to chew
  what must have seemed the Hand of Death.
Our intent was never murder though;
    we only hoped to see

    the push   and pull

      of ancient Instinct.
    So we'd pinch the tail,
      let the lizard hang
for what must have seemed an age to him,
    —even now I forever see the spine
  serpentining, twisting up, curling round—
      and thus we'd watch the lizard swing,
hang like a pendant orb dangling
    from a golden chain

till the tapered, armored thread
would suddenly snap, severed
from the body main—
and in my hand the tail.
It would remain,
as the body fell and smacked the ground—

Now the lizard darts
back down dark,
thin stony fissures;

and there above,
awed by absence,
silent we stand,

staring at the
blank forged
by lizard's loss

or should I
say a forgery
of lizard loss

for his image
& his tail
remained & still

remain buried
deep within
my lizard brain.

Artemis Goes Hunting

for Gary Snyder

gods made by human hands are not gods at all
—ST PAUL TO THE SILVERSMITHS OF EPHESUS

Wormwood is sacred to Artemis. Narrow leaves glow silver in her moonlight.
—GARY SNYDER

When the goddess busked into the ruins
and asked me to dance right there where
Paul had hectored artisans after thinking
too long & hard on Praxiteles's busty votive
Artemis, I was whispering to myself,

> What does one say in such a spot
> where a great river's been reduced
> to reeds and lilies in a ditch?
> What does one say to a lover
> whose temple lies in ruins?

So we waltzed through wormwood
while Artemis smelled of lavender, milk
and venison, a scent which stirred
not just thoughts of venery
but that no man's hand had made her
and Gary's line that the Greek *artem*
means *earring*
as well as *dangle*
—and I risked whispering in her ear:
an ear is just an ear without an earring;

her reply was a toothy lobe nip,
and a tongue probe into its parent
which eased our fall into the tall grass
spread along the dark dry bed

of the late *Kücuck Menderez* river,
where we lay beneath the stars.

Then through the silent dark
the huntress sighed: *I know of arts
in which an ear is more than just an ear*
        and with a sudden blow,
straight like an adder,
through the long grass,
she slid and drew me to her under
   that silver slivered moon.

I thought this can't be Artemis—
I've always heard it is the hunt
and not the kill which is the art
   she truly loves. . .oh god,
I thought, this can't be her.

At which the moon raced behind a cloud,
   and of a sudden she disappeared.

Now I'm left dangling from her memory,
forced to hunt for mortal ears that
I might pierce with this quaint old lay
about our love between the lilies
and the reeds, about our tenderness
above the watercress and moss—
      oh, love among the ruins.

Family Recipe

There are secrets in all families.
—GEORGE FARQUHAR, *The Beaux' Strategem*

Love and more brings her back to this aspen board
where she watched her mother's hands years before;
   now my wife's midriff rises slow and sure
     like the cakes and goods she bakes.

Now, in August, before the heavy harvest
   there's time for pies.
With hands supple and strong as stems
   she skeins the skin from fleshy rounds
of stippled greens and russets
   that fall in seamless shining whorls—

Good apples make good filling, she says
   as I touch her belly's swell and palm
its gravid fullness adding, *Filling is the better portion.*

Without good crust a pie is not a pie.
     Flour, water, shortening, salt—simple recipe
the secret's in the mixing, she shines a smile.

You should write it out, I reply,
  Promises or words or recipes just spoken
You know they always get forgotten.

By doing this I'll hand it on to him or her
   like mama's did with her. . .and hers with her.
   You can't put down some kinds of love.

So love and word of mouth endure.
   Still I have to write it:
Flour, shortening, water, salt,
   fruit picked before the fall.

Endnotes (What I Didn't Write)

All happy families resemble one another, but each unhappy family is unhappy in its own way.

—LEO TOLSTOY

What I didn't write is that I'm a mean eye in winter looking through a jagged pane of ice. Beneath this beak, below this shattered looking glass, shriveled skins appear and mis-appear. Who am I? I am the magpie, a bird of prey reputed to feed off irises and offal, a scavenger, the kind of which in winter, after apple picking, devours fruit that lands beyond the cider heap, windfalls which otherwise might get forgotten.

And I didn't write that Cait's mother was already thinking of leaving that summer, even after forty years of wed-lock; she longed to leave the farm even as I sat wondering in the long grass, a cultivated green which was once a dirt patch where my wife mixed mud cakes as a kid.

The eye wanders and makes its own importances & unimportances, but seldom we know why. To this the boredom-stricken magpie must reply:

The eye with which you see reality must constantly be changed, compounded.

And I didn't write that I sat coveting her father's fruited orchard while he was out mowing pastures of lucerne. Or that the reek of half-soured silage wafted by while Cait was straddling a rough concrete floor that sent varicose spidering like purple prose along her calves.

Nor did I note that weevils and shrikes had spoilt all the granny smiths and because freestones were barely cleaving the line between ripe and rot, she was fixing not *apple* pie as I said but rather *peach* pie with my prepubescent daughter.

And that day, as they mixed the family recipe and Cait handed down to our daughter what she came to call the gnosis of menses, it seems my only interest was witnessing the sight of sweet gravensteins flowing on windfall streams of light.

And I also didn't write that I-5 snakes across the San Joaquin a mile or less from there, a place where, when Cait was twelve, Caltrans cut an asphalt scar across the belly of the valley so now you always hear the drone of traffic. Of this she likes to recall how, after the interstate came through, she imagined the distant sound of trucks and cars was the whirr of honey bees distilling.

Nor did I write that just off Exit-7, two miles from that house where her folks reared twelve kids, stands Pinkey's Truck Stop, a greasy spoon where waitresses on their smoke break crawl up into curtained sleeper cabs of big rig drivers.

And here's something I couldn't have written before the November rains of that bitter fall gave way to winter fogs among the tule reeds—

a false vision of haiku I'd first dreamed on Lone Mountain in 1982:

> A new colleague scans / my bookshelves while in the streets / dogs sniff dogs' asses

How is it that I can write this now, but couldn't in the days before the heavy harvest? Perhaps it's that we never know when it's time to write *finis* to the pastoral. Or is it that I and the magpie sense all songs have just one true season and that the skins of some can stomach a skein of only so much suffering? Maybe it's just as Rilke says:

Everything is gestation and then bringing forth.

So this is what I didn't write, though something like it somewhere keeps happening, almost all the time:

> a lonely woman makes plans   to leave
> her man who's mowing in the garden;
> years later   she will wake one winter
> and find herself in bed   dying alone,
>   holding nobody's hand,
> not even her estranged daughter's

who (out across the Great Divide),
is too busy   at this very moment
pushing out a lovely stained and russet head
between all the necessary mess of urine and feces—
   a woman who's too busy
(straddling that line between death and life)
to care for luxuries   of absence and artifice
and yells at baby's literate (but oh so clueless) father
   who keeps telling her to breathe.

To this Cait and the magpie really should reply,

Would you mind shutting the f— up.

All this was there
just ripening and rottening
imperceptibly unleaving
as in countless other seasons
of voluptuous return,
before the heavy harvest,
waiting for that late season's
scattering of leaves
with their grating
and their tuneless turning
we were all just waiting,
waiting with the magpie
   for the fall—
   the fall that comes
   before the spring.

No More Story Time

In your fondest memory
The scent of baking pies
Soothes your lizard brain
As mother reads to you.
Your are four, cozied on her lap
As she tells how Red Riding Hood's
Terrible travail turns out oh so well—
      a genuine fairy tale.

Later, she will dress your German Shepherd
In brother's jeans
& name him Woodcutter.
This is a spectacle you still love
To recall as so much fun.
This is her happy time, before the migraines
Before the half dozen other children
Before the wolf bared his ivoried teeth
And masqueraded as your mother,
Your messed up mama who's still too busy
Playing Wicked Stepmother
To ever read to you again.

Hansel Can't You See, Gretel's Got PTSD?

Why must you keep tilling the boneyard of memory?
What I hate most, Gretel, is finding you wandering at midnight naked
Among the trees. You stammer and stutter: *Look, the oaks walk*

About, but the crab is on the loose. Don't turn your back, brother.
To mow down the life of another—you keep reminding me
Sister—*there's no love greater than a girl who kills for a brother.*

True, you hoodwinked & baked the hungry hag for my sake.
Sure, I'm grateful, but what's eating you is murder. Without that Grand
Guignol playing in your skull, I'd recall nothing from our *Alptraum*—

Not how she yanked out your hair in clumps, not the cage,
Not the sweets and pastry feasts, nor the chicken-bone trick.
Forgetting heals, you know, but curiosity kills. No greater love?

Look what I've endured for your sake: your weeping and wailing
Under the crimson moon, your spitting and hissing, pyromaniac games,
And morning after morning I can hardly drag you out of bed.

The worst, though: having to sit and watch with you
That interminable DVD of Humperdinck's opera over
And over, seeing you smile, shoving her through the iron door.

And I despise your filthiness, your snarled hair,
Your *need to talk about it* then your refusal to talk
Because *nobody really understands*. Why the hell can't you purge

The past, give me back my sweet *Schwesterlein*?
Sometimes life gets so crooked crazy I fear I'll find you bleeding
At the brook, your wrists slashed with broken glass
               (for we've hidden the knives & razors)

And you just staring at your face in grimaced water.
Some days I wish I could crawl back into the cage
Or that the old hag had ended it all right there—

Finished my life in a furnace flash. Then you'd have no
Incessant need to kvetsch. Better for me to be a pile
Of sticky ash, gritty bone. All I know for certain now:

The yarn of living happily ever after with you and Papa,
Is just one more propagandist's trick.

Sloe Gin, Slow Suicide

1

Sitting in my garden of a sunny autumn afternoon.
September aspens are dressed in dappled light
the kind of luminescence you only seem to see
when you're good & lubed, the kind of light you feel
deep within the vein and in the hurt heart's core,
a changeling light in which your pain begins to ebb
into a softening pulse that flows and spiders like
purpled alpenglow on red rock canyon walls.

Now I'm feeling loose and fine, like a boozer soused
on Bourbon Street, as the tingle at my spine
and in my toes says, *Throw me something mistah,*
   something sweet and sloe
so as not to break the spell and mystic flow.

And though the mind says, *you've had your fill*
the will wants otherwise and pleads:
Why not make a temporary heaven
out of your private hidden little hell?
So between my lips I start to swill
another gin and tonic—
my fourth in fifty minutes.

In that fading light I then begin to see
through quinine and the spirits, the quidditas
of things unseen comes dropping sloe
and pure as claritas like all the gin
drained from my empty glass.

I see again again so many many men,
gifted men in slow suicidal moods:
men who had no reason to desire

death, no good reason that the world could tell,
(at least no reason that reading stones or bones
ever would reveal), and yet a lethal mustard seed
took root in their heart's core and grew
into a Judas tree from which they hung
a knotted rope, slipped their necks, then
slowly cinched until they couldn't breathe.

2

Here's a little *bas relief* carved from the poison wood
       of the hangman's tree:
Ten years back I saw my jocund Uncle Jack
pull back the pasteboard mask and strike the perfect
pose of a man bent on slow suicide.

From three one day until two a.m. the next, we sat
at Jack's Jalisco hacienda on Lake Chapala's
poisoned shore and drank enough to fell six lesser men:
sixteen Coronas (my five to his eleven), a partial fifth
of Cuervo Gold, the dregs of the obligatory Bombay Sapphire
I'd carted south to pay my board, a demi carafe of rot gut brandy,
and, God knows why, a partial jug of "imported" Carlo Rossi.

At first we smiled much and laughed.
But as day gave way to Venus rising
in the west, I said to Jack, *That's Hesperus,*
it's already evening. We should take it easy, Unc.
His reply: *Only drink as much, son, as whatever ails you.*

When the sun sank behind the drought parched hills,
the world went dark (but for the light of Hesperus in the west)
and in that witching hour before the gibbous moon
rose over his hacienda garden, old Jack began to brood.

With tongue envenomed, ready for the kill,
he skewered four former wives for near an hour
then keened failed schemes for making filthy lucre.
What tholed Jack most, though, was how with boozing
and his tongue he'd ostracized his kids.

But with the rising of the moon
Jack's fit of choler lifted.
He raised his glass and measured out
a toast magpied from Lord Byron:

I would to Heaven I were so much Clay
as I am blood, bone, gism, marrow, passion 'cause at least
the past were past away…And for the future
but I say this reeling having got drunk exceedingly today…
For Godsake let's stop this idle chatter…and drink!

Drink, non-stop, we did until at one he scooped
a kitten from a patio tile, and cradling the calico
in his arm's crook he stroked the kit
beneath the humpback moon
as if it were his baby, then began to croon,
Daddy's gonna buy you a mocking bird
and if that mocking bird don't sing…

As I poured another round, Jack stroked and sang
some more and we swilled the last of that Lodi *tinta*.
But two a.m. he rose to spend his waters.
The moon stood overhead, light bathed the garden.
And just as soon as he'd turned the corner, I heard
a crash across the yard. He'd fallen off the stoop.
His jeans were wet; his Mexican bride stood sobbing.

Jack was weeping too. He didn't want my help.
So I just turned and went to bed, left him
with the kit cradled in his arms—
crushed, as if it slept.

Heirloom Photograph

> *If you are interested in scars I can show you some very interesting ones but I would rather tell you about grasshoppers.*
> —NICK ADAMS IN "A Way You'll Never Be"

In a reprint of a photo posted on my laptop screen
    struts my grandpa, a raw recruit just sixteen.
Notice how he stands smart and stract
    in a uniform stylish yet oversized
        and by the ladies prized
(despite its common medium-brown drabness).

See how he smiles shouldering the gravid rucksack
    that he'll bear across the Western Front
from the Somme to Vimy Ridge.

It's the jaw, though, that always numbs
my nuts—see how it juts
    as if to say to the demon Hun,
Bring it on Jerry boy, I dare your sorry ass.

Later in the labyrinth of the trenches
he'll shed the rucksack
from his back
as he runs & pronks about
the redoubt dodging minatory
five-nines & corpses bloating in the sun,
hopping like a hunted hopper
who somehow always finds some shade.
Oh lucky hopper slips his rear
just beyond the shit-show sickle
mowing so much hay.

Note the photo doesn't show his fright—
that's the face of battle that almost always gets forgotten,

the oh-shit face that says he's crapped his knickers
as he carts dead-end dispatches day & night
from colonel to captain—again, again, again.

In the photo he just smiles smiles smiles.
                    Should fresh recruits look otherwise?
What good's a greenhorn grunt who smells his own demise?

Absent from the photo too is grandpa's brother,
       age twenty-seven, a courier who wears the same
drab uniform, the usual medium-brown affair.
But for the dog tag stats stamped upon the rim
    of a few paltry medals awarded postmortem
        (760520 PTE J. Taggart)
I know next to nothing of this phantom kin.

I want grandpa's and his brother's rest
    to be more than silence though
      so I'll sing their song of suffering:
One day as gramps trailed
his brother he blinked not once but twice
    as five-nine fragments sliced
        clean through parapets & gunnysacks.

Until gramps died from the disease called slow suicide,
    the curse of working men & gutted soldiers,
a pyrotechnic trauma show of haywire synapses fired
   near every night in the minefield of his neural paths.

Here's the nightly horror show he saw
   till his liver finally caved
    like a fish rotting in the head:

      first a flame-red flash
      quickens the retina
      as a smooth shrapnel

      axe scythes all
      within its path;

        then a white-hot
        fragment crops
        the shaved carrot top
        of dear brother's
        patriotic head—
        and of a sudden
        brother John
        (sweet, sweet Jack)
        is oh so dead.

And in that vision smooth and clean
    as a mower glides through long grass green—
  a nightly déjà vu of a shrapnel blade that felled for good
      sweet John in that ridgeline field of mud—
in that unkind, uncouth, ungodly sight
    Grandpa's photogenic jaw came unhinged,
        unhinged forever.

Heorot

Give us a house to wreck
　　　　　We'll tear it down by heck.
　　—HECKLE & JECKLE, *House Busters*

War favored and fortuned　famous Hrothgar.
Kith and kin admired him　brimmed his cadres,
(nubile fighters gathered)　a force formed
into a massive army.　So his mind veered
to hall-making:　he meted out orders
for followers to fashion　a great mead-hall
that would ever be　a wonder of the world;
it would hold his throne　& there he would
gift young & old　with God-given goods—

　　　　　…And soon it stood there
finished and sturdy　for servant & squire to admire,
hero of halls　Heorot it was called
by the lord whose word　was always law.
He broke no promises　and paid out rings
and torques at table.　The fortress towered,
its gables wide and high,　but it always waited,
watched for a wanton burning.　Doom waits too
and emerge it will:　fatal instinct is un-noosed,
loosed among in-laws,　blood-lust runs riot.

　　　　　　—AFTER THE BEOWULF SCOP

Het Huis

By then day had broken everywhere, but here it was still night—no, more than night.
  —PLINY THE YOUNGER'S DESCRIPTION OF THE ERUPTION OF MOUNT VESUVIUS, THE FUMES OF WHICH KILLED HIS UNCLE, PLINY THE ELDER

In Holland eighteen is the legal age for working whores. Sitting in her display window a *meisje* from a former colony cups and circles her ebony breasts. Barely eighteen, the girl yawns behind her spotless shop windowpane. I glance at her, then at my daughter. I can recall what I knew at eighteen, but wonder how much I knew at eleven. Kelsey pretends to ignore the drab. *Papa, how much further to Anne Frank's house?* I change the subject: *Have you ever read the word prostitute?*

* * *

Rain falls from a clay-and-mortar sky that, for weeks now, has shrouded Amsterdam like a winding sheet. Though the calendar says late June, the air feels like fall. Rain every day this month. And in the street, all I hear beyond the harlot's cry is talk of global warming, immigration blight, and the price of petrol.

* * *

We can't find Anne Frank's secret annex, her refuge called *het achterhuis*. Lost and out of place, my daughter and I keep walking. On Prinsengrachtstraat, we skirt offal: shattered beer bottles and condoms lie on cobblestones like so many shards of spent lust. Down below the quay, in the stew of a slime-green canal, Amstel bottles and *frites* wrappers rock and bob in the clash of barge-wakes. And last night at dinner, my queer leftist friend from Maastricht told us *Amsterdam is vies…just dirty and shot to hell.* Twenty years ago, he called my rich, conservative friends from Haarlem fascists. Besieged now by this "filthy" postmodern tide, they've all lost their minds, defend Pim Fortuyn's ultra-right assault on "backward Islam," and say, *Holland isn't what it used to be—they've filled it with their drek and decadence.*

* * *

And I whisper to myself what an unkind memory it is that only glances rearward. Still I can't help but cast back to 1982, a summer when I wandered for hours along these canals, enraptured by their green waters—*grachten* waters and canal banks that then seemed so leafy-with-love. I knew my way around. But in the chill of here-and-now, I'm dazed and out of place. We keep circling these canal rings, passing heroin addicts and dozens of boy tricks as they stand waiting, shivering in a slant of rain.

* * *

Kelsey peers into the downpour. The low, joyless sky moves me to consider the time of our demise. When will we die…five, ten, thirty, fifty years? Still waiting for Kelsey to answer my question, my thoughts turn to some poet way across the ocean who keeps churning out well-measured verse about everything but the actual mess. Why does no one write anymore like Pliny the Younger and his uncle Pliny the Elder, that most Roman natural historian who said, *Vita vigilia est…to be alive means to be awake*? That was before Vesuvius got him. Pliny the Younger, both nephew and protégé of the Elder, recounts what killed his uncle was not a fifteen-hundred-degree tide of bloody lava. Curiosity and the gas got him.

* * *

I repeat my question, holding the sad notes of that strange word a little longer: Have you ever read the word *pros-ti-tute?* Kelsey squints through tiny spectacles fogged by the damp. She shakes her head. When we turn a corner, we find *het achterhuis*, then climb like pilgrims, curious to see the half-lit attic where the little Jewish author kept her own vigil, letter by strange letter, until she too was dragged into the dark.

Tonight My Father's Dying

let the silver chord snap
and moon fall into the sea—
      let morning come;

    let milkmen roam in the street;
tell the old gal: put out his winding sheet—
      let morning come;

let magpies wake us from sleep
and tears be dried by the sun—
      let morning come;

let morning come,
and after break of day—
      the light of morning sun

Rust

Lay not up for yourselves treasures upon earth, where moth and rust doth corrupt, and where thieves break through and steal.

—MATTHEW 6:19–21

Rust ruins metal everywhere. Dad, you would've fought that line and said, *What kind of weak-assed poet imagined that?* So rust helps me remember you and how as a kid I'd often scoop from wet earth rust-riven soup cans, hod pails, fenders, coffee tins—only to see their centers buckle and collapse between my small hands; this happened so often & everywhere, I see perfectly, even now, paper-thin flakes of burnt sienna dissipate, rain down & fade into soaked green earth. How's it feel now to see, to sing these shards of memory? How did the *actual* feel back then when I didn't know how to say *disintegrate?* Like finding a kitten runt smothered beneath his mother, or like spotting blood on your unworn wedding dress; or catching you know who in bed with your brother's wife, but somehow I can't quite bring myself to go so far to say it's the same as watching cousin David duck under the water's surface for the fifth and final time. When I was young, Dad, you kept that huge old axle grease pail on the workbench shelf; that bucket brimmed with shiny nuts and bolts, a few rusted nails. In that pail's heft and cold hardness, I hoped that here was something that finally might break the back of time. But Dad, you're dead a month now: four weeks since you havered on your winding sheet, spewing what calcined cancer nurses call *coffee grounds,* then you gave up the ghost saying, *Let's get this thing done.* For two days your corpse stiffened, curing in cold storage. Then, in a furnace flash, you were reduced to nothing more than a pile of sticky ash, gritty bone. Here's how we starve magpie and the worm. Ashes to ashes, rust to dust.

Garden Plots

Fuck her fucking flowers, Gicamdi cried as I tried
to make a point about the pastoral in Walcott and Césaire.
Daily people were dying in the streets & gutters.
Pastoral's just one more way of taking cover
in the course of taking over.

Fostered in the rain shadow of Kilimanjaro
but ivy-league trained,
my prof railed like this for near an hour
against the wealthy white woman he'd heard
on Radio Kenya during a brutal year of revolution.

From somewhere in her compound, somewhere
behind iron-grated windows and bits of glass
grouted into the fortress walls around her house
that idiot lady rambled on and on complaining
to the talk show host about her troubles growing bougainvillea.

Every spring since then, Gicamdi's echoed in my ear
and I've repressed my flower fetish.
Who needs to add more guilt
when there's guilt enough to go around?
And I've come to half believe what Ho Chi Minh
said about his need for more poets
who could lead a charge, sharpen bayonets.

What with war, though, shattering Iraq
and scattering her children from Oaxes to the River Jordan,
what with sloughing glaciers raising sea level,
and me still grieving for my old man
who's been planted in the earth
pushing daisies for two years now
I start to wonder what's the harm

of a bit of color,
a little excess in the garden.

So this sheepish spring I'm raising flowers.
Years past, I justified my garden plots by rearing apples,
chives, tomatoes, cucumbers for pickling & canning.
I rarely saw much fruit for all my labor:
this sub-alpine elevation stunts all such growing.
Now I'm splurging, sowing a few perennials—
cornflowers, coreopsis, columbine—
but mounds of annuals, the kind of water-wasting
hopeless blooms that in these mountain parts
will fade in fall and not revive next spring:
cosmos, sweet peas with their sexy
scent and tendrils, and bleeding heart.

With every toss of seed I start to feel a hint of hope—
just a momentary flash; isn't that the only honest hope
when folks keep falling in the streets, falling
by the thousands in Mosul, Jalalabad, Calcutta?
And when at last the flowers bloom,
that color splash is cruel—it comes so slow,
then quickly passes; for in high country parts
like these even when it's spring,
      winter waits and watches.

BLACK FOREST, COLORADO (ELEVATION 8013 FT)
   JUNE 2006

Peace Lily
(with Peace Walls Leading to a Haiga)

1
Good fences make good neighbors
So chimes the grey-haired poet.
      But what of walls?

2
Sometimes it takes a wall to keep the peace
So say the Ulster Irish…that's exactly
What I saw standing on the Falls Road, Belfast,
Where that straight thoroughfare of spite flanks
The Shankill Road. There it towered, an air-borne
Wall for peace, formed from iron, brick, and stone,
Plus shards of broken glass, whatever they could grab
To launch their peace-complacent wall higher,

Higher into the Ulster sky toward the British heaven—
Each day before my foreign eyes it rose and rose
To stretch its stated end: corral the hate,
Defend against the dragon and keep the peace.

3

And in the middle of the picture sits a single
Lily, a lily in a painted pot at the center
Of a space made safe, secure by surrounding
Walls—imposing, four-square forms wrought
From brick and rock and mortar—stiff stuff set
Firm and tough enough to keep the peace.

4

The broken wall . . . burning tower
                And Agamemnon dead
And Humpty Dumpty sat on a wall
    Humpty Dumpty had a great fall.

5

Since so much depends
Upon a painted lily in a pot
Safe within its walls,
Strange it seems how no
One really sees the flower
Yet the peace it promises
That's the power that they love
(It's what they lack and long for)
So they cheer the lily's unseen
Blossoming—a gift of hope,
A hope that drives out fear,
For this they cheer, raising
Signs and songs unto the lily
In the little painted pot
Safe within the walls four-square.

6

Three times Achilles chased him
Round the walls and towers

Ringing Ilium, three times Hector
Passed his wife and kin atop
The ramparts gasping, groaning
As the son of Peleus gained ground
On the fleeing prince. Then the fourth
Time round those walls sorrow swept
The crowd who watched their lover, son
And brother fall—
                Death's dark curtain dropped…
And round the walls, Achilles dragged the prince
Dragged his corpse face down behind his glinting
Chariot through the bloodied mud and dirt.

                7

Sometimes it takes a certain kind
Of wall to strike what's called a
Separate peace, at least that's what
I mean to say to end this painful
Chain of word and image verse—

                8

So in that spirit here's a *haiga*,
A picture and a poem in tandem
About a man named George,
George Yamasaki born in Osaka
But raised in Northern California,
A man they tried to cage and break
Behind a fence of coiled concertina wire,
A man whose soul they tried to snuff
Stealing his nursery, trashing his orchards,
Torching his home when war broke out in '41;
But George refused to break, refused to die,
Refused to fade away like lilies of the valley—
And when the war was done, home he came
To the rolling hills round Auburn,
Then set to work raising walls again,
Rebuilt his life stacking quartz and granite
Not just to feed his boys and wife…No,

George showed that though they tried
To bend and bow him like a bonsai, to cage
Him like a magpie, he refused to bow or break:

    Back from camp at Tule Lake
      Yamasaki built these walls
    Freestones in mortar

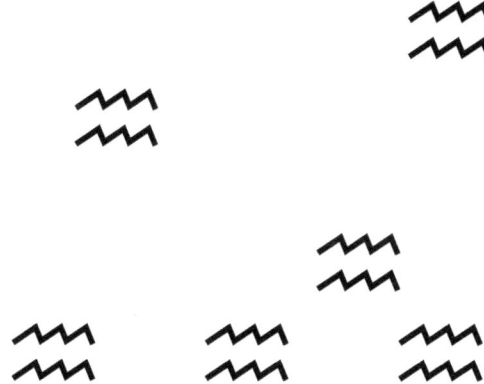

Magpie Sings on Sun Mountain

Your dead shall live; *their bodies shall rise.*
You who dwell in the dust, awake and sing for joy!
For your dew is a dew of light,
And the land of shades gives birth.

—ISAIAH 26:16-19

Once in his life a man ought to concentrate his mind upon the remembered earth, I believe. He ought to give himself up to a particular landscape in his experience, to look at it from as many angles as he can, to wonder about it, to dwell upon it. He ought to imagine that he touches it with his hands at every season and listens to the sounds that are made upon it.

—N. SCOTT MOMADAY, *The Way to Rainy Mountain*

What follows charts a migration and transformation into my Magpie and our subsequent escape from the massacre by means of a Sun Mountain ascent. Why? Twenty-four years of Air Force service, forever wars, the prospect of global ecological collapse, the dark angel of history, or perhaps just the need for a change of scenery and a limbic system reset…sometimes one needs to take cover, seek refuge in a good place. This poem sequence takes its inspiration from two classic mad-man-in-the-wild tales, Han Shan's Cold Mountain *poems and the Middle Irish* Buile Suibhne. *In a few places, I have unabashedly magpied these ancient works, scavenging bits and pieces of translated fragments from these classics. In this I count myself an heir of Basho, following in his footsteps along the kado, the Tao of poetry, just as he followed in Saigyō's footsteps, walking up old ghost paths, seeking the spirit of the ancients in the shared, steep mountain ascent that is poetry.*

In the midst of our forever wars, three concussive shouts went up as the herded forces bugled, bellowed like rutting elk. When Suibhne Mac (who is partly me) heard this din together with its echoing between the heaven's clouds, the front range, and the dome of the firmament, he gazed at the Mountain of the Sun, and did a doubletake, whereupon turbulence and shadow and rage and giddiness and skipped heartbeats and frenzy and levitations, instability, unrest and dis-ease filled him. Likewise disgust with every foul place he'd been invaded his heart, but also desire for every good place, every *querencia* he'd never known. With that, the warp spasm set in:

> His fingers froze stiff
> His wheels shimmied
> His heart palpitated
> His senses overloaded
> His vision clouded
> His spear and sword fell
> Unsheathed from his hands

Then as a cursed, migrated soul, Suibhne Mac skedaddled from the battle, not as a man anymore, but as a bird of the air, in madness and incredulity. Flying out of the murderous into the miraculous, he began to sing a song, a scattered song but one that sent up some semblance of solace:

I skip, skim, dip and climb past ruined, rubbled cities—
Suburban stone heaps, middens of history.
Derelict defenses, high and low, stand watch all around:
Radar, antiaircraft batteries, missile silos, satellite relays
And millions of burial plots to quarantine angry ancestors,
Spirits long gone, forgotten. But just as many tombs, too,
Waiting for the living dead, great and small.
In an alleyway, the rustle of a tumbleweed mimics
An empty plastic sack and the voice of a hacked spirit tree
Cries out. Can I only sigh at so much life squandered, lost—
Who will ever see the sun again or sing on its holy mountain?

After the bird-man fled the fight and then the ruined city, his feet rarely touched the ground, so fleet he flew. When he did touch down on paydirt, he shook no dew from the long-stemmed bear grass or the piercing yucca because his step was light and nimble. From that headlong course, he did not veer. So straight and true and fast he flew, he left unvisited neither plain, nor field, nor mountain scar, nor bog, nor thicket, nor marsh, nor hogback hill, nor holloweg, nor dense-sheltering wood. He travelled such, until he reached the banks of a cutthroat pool on Bear Creek, where he lit on a chokecherry tree near the aspen stand at the margin of a lizard seep. There he saw, darting about, shadowy shapes of trout, the cutthroat kind, believed to be extinct. But the Bear Creek clan of fish refused to die. There they were—to marvel at, as they'd been for ten thousand years, all rose-moled and speckled in pied beauty.

In the aspen shade, all his senses opened, refreshed. Slowly he felt himself becoming new, becoming something strange and wonderful, becoming well again. Still the route was no less rocky, and since singing smooths the way, he made a song about the steep journey that lay ahead of him:

> Going to the mountain—poetry
> Going to the mountain—let me be
> Yeah, I'm going to the mountain—
> Going to the mountain—poetry
> Going to the mountain—let it be
> Going to the mountain
>   Set me free
> Going to the mountain—poetry

Once he staggered onto the holy mountain, he dreamed into being many other songlines so he'd remember what ought never get forgotten, so he might remember the way.

Escaped from the abattoir
My magpie who is partly me
Reaches the forest margin
Where we ascend the path
Of magpiety, the way up
    Sun Mountain,
The path that is no path,
The way never ending.

Folded foothills rise and fall
As far as these magpie eyes
Can see on a hundred-mile day.

Scree and glacial debris
Litter steep slopes; cricks,
Rivulets and rills well
From rocks and hills.
Like the place in flowers
Where pollen rests,
The east slope cradles
The sound of melted
Snow running fast.

Here below the tree line
In spruce and fir shade
Where lichen flourishes
The air's so cool and thin
It tastes like liberation.

Over the lower western slope
Above eskered moraines
I learn to glide and smile again.

I dip and sometimes even soar—
The savor of wind and moss
In my mouth and nose gives
Rise to green thoughts
In a green land…to peace.
Thoughts of the world below
All wrapped in silence,
Stillness. Marriage of mountain
And sky blows my mind.

My days are filled with wandering
Across the mountain, wondering why
It took so long to ditch the minefield
Of memory, the catalogue of killing.

Many are the miracles scattered,
Strewn on the way to magpiety.
Instead of flying I sometimes claw
And creep up *Tava*'s face—
So new and weak my wings are.

The mountaintop peeks in and out
Of view, blocked by crags, hoodoos,
Glacial boulders higher than huge houses.
So I seek small creases of passage.
Between a havoc of boulders,
Towering mansions of stone gap
Just enough for me to slink and slide
Lizard-like through fissured rock.

Then the narrow trail opens
Out onto a field in bloom,
A field of luscious larkspur,
Lupin, monkshoods, gentians,
Buttercups and carpets of snow
Lilies. Who needs to summit *Tava*
When you can loaf in wildflower beds?

Naked as a jay I came into the world,
Fifty-five years ago, between
Feces and urine, was I born.
Millions of miles I've traveled now—
Along rivers churning, blood-boltered
By clay, beyond borders where brigands lay
In wait, I drank *chibuku* with war vets.
I read book upon book, sang the annals,
Studied Sanskrit and Dari. All in vain,
Searching, moving always seeking a path
To the fountain of fullness.
But today I'm holding still,
Nothing doing on Sun Mountain,
Loafing, feeling well above average.

At my feet, on the cobbled riprap
A dragonfly catches her breath.
I could eat her
So famished am I.
She tilts her head with her compound
Eye throwing a look my way
That shows no fear, just compassion.
Looking, I recall, is the better portion,
Not eating. Oh, that I could see as she—
Through a hundred lenses of love.

I've come to see the Earth as Earth
Must see itself, which means my eyes
Pry into cracks and hard rock crevices,
Peer into luminous, clear watered
Loughs and tarns where I look for what
Seems forever, but I know I've only just
Begun, have hardly started seeing.

Once I was an officer armed with books
And a Beretta. I have served two masters:
I taught in the west but that won few prizes
I fought in the east with fat cat colonels
I guzzled the arts of war, the arts of peace
Now I wonder if peace really is the end of art.
Now I'm an old bird, what's left of my life
No one will notice; it isn't worth an ink cartridge.

At dusk, on the verge of an esker field,
I spot a lone pine, one bent & twisted,
Arched, aimed at the summit.
Some might say this tree was jachelt,
Krummholzed by easterly winds.
But I know better—the ancient ones
Trained this ponderosa into a bow shape,
A living horseshoe standing sideways
For centuries, a living sculpture
Where tonight I'll sleep in the crook
Of its upper curve. Who needs a mattress
When a pine robed in starlight is your bed?

To sleep on the branch of a pine tree
Is bliss, it brings on blessings,
Like sleeping in a spirit tower.
But sometimes my bed is hardpan,
My blanket star shine, so my slumber's
Fitful. There are times I waken angry
At the world, unwell in mind and body,
Hopping mad like a cricket stoppered
In a bottle, raging as if a screw's been
Twisted in my forehead. Then walking's
The only sure cure for me,
Walking or hearing the sound of water.

A ghost walker or Han Shan (or was it Dogen?)
Whispered in my ear: *The color of the mountain
Is the Buddha's body, the sound of water
Is his sacred speech.* So when others say
The only way up Sun Mountain's alone,
I scoff. The ancient ones are everywhere.
They talk—
To them I listen when I walk.
If we'd only learn to look and listen,
With us they'll always walk the way.
Now I hear them sighing through
Quaking aspen leaves, whispering
In the rutted path, voices rising
From the dust. Can you hear them
Too? They're soughing in my ears.

Here are words sung on Earth's altar,
The wisdom of mountain song:

Wait and watch, hold still.
Then and only then you'll see
The tree, the bird in the bush
For what they are, not what
You dream they ought to be.

Oh, lungs of the Earth, be praised.

One night after dusk, the bird-man found himself bivouacked on a slippery slope of mountain scree bathed in moonlight. There a terrible apparition arose. Bleeding headless torsos swirled around and decapitated heads—seven scruffy, goat-bearded heads—bansheed, bouncing to and fro over the mountainside. When he approached them, he heard them yapping:

—He is bonkers, said the first head.
—A lunatic from down on the plains, said the second.
—Harry him to hell, said the third.
—May the hunt be long lived, said the fourth.

—Hound him till doomsday, said the fifth.
—The other two said nothing.

The heads rose like a kettle of vultures, circling round him, but the bird-man darted away in front, skimming the peak above the timberline, then back down into the trees; no matter how wide the meadows and valleys were, he managed to stay in front of the hunt.

> The heads haunted him,
> Hunted him heinously
> Lapping and baying
> Their hot breath always
> At his back, snapping, yelping,
> Neighing, squealing.
> The heads sniffed at his calves,
> Licked his thighs, tapped his
> Shoulder, nuzzled his neck,
> But he gave them the slip
> And they crashed into tree-trunks
> And crag-faces, then plummeted
> Like cataracts, and he ditched
> Them in a dervish swirl of mist.

Suibhne's scrape with the flying heads gave him pause, made him think again about always praising marvels, miracles. So he made a song that carved out space for some of the murderous:

> Violent is the world
> Violent is the volcano
> In my breast
> And violent the verse
> That must be sung—
> That's how we truly see
> And salve the wound.

> How can you stay angry walking,
> Listening to the ancient ones?
> Sighing, soughing through the trees.

They soothe, smooth my nerves.
How can you be angry at the whiff
Of rain on sun-strewn riprap,
The tang of raw pinon nut tugging
At my tongue? How can you be
Cross napping in a field of falling
Stars or watching Hesperus set below
A crescent moon? Or scornful seeing
A cutthroat rise and watching cotton-
Wood snows pile up in June? Out
Here anger's pretty much impossible.

The pines hum
But there's no breeze.
Life spirit rises from the pines.
From the pines comes spirit life,
Ruah. World's refreshed, renewed.
Oh, lungs of the Earth, be praised.

The way to my magpie nest is luminous,
A slipstream of light and shadow carried
On thermal winds sired by Sun Mountain,
(Oh, *Tava*), the center of the world, where
Magpie lives and dies and rises again each
Day. As *Tava* shines on *Tava* so multiplies
The great light of day, oh light that fills
My heart, the light that fills the world.

Some say solitude's the thing—
Seek treasure at the mountaintop,
Alone. But ever since I summitted
By myself, I've longed to share
Sun Mountain with anyone who cares:
Kids, warriors, blind beggars. I lead
Them halfway up, then I leave them
On a ledge. That's the only way

They'll learn to really see and scale
Sun Mountain. On their own, they'll walk
Into the soul of *Tava-kaavi*
And find there the power-of-solitude.

Living on the plains, mind troubled
Heart troubled, all I did was lament
Lost time. I tasted many potions,
Brews, medicinals to calm my spirit,
Bolster my bone-house: bistorts
As a sorry stay against scurvy,
Snake root for aches and pains,
Root of Canby's lovage to sweeten
The voice, valerians to calm the nerves.
Did any of that add one cubit
To my life's span or slow the weaver's
Shuttle? Did any of that cure the first
Hurt, the cause of all my ills?

But I've found my good place now,
My safe spot in the ring, my *querencia*—

A white quartz medicine wheel
Dazzling like the moonlit mist up there
That scarfs the crest trail by the summit.
Down here, too, halfway up the peak,
The sacred grove and golden meadow
Where the holy wheel stands, they all
Glint in the solstice moon shine.

Beyond the sacred wheel, I've found
A salve to heal whatever ails me:
A bent and lovely spirit tower,
Where a grooved scar snakes round
The stripped and gyred trunk,
Like a molting uroboros unwound.
At the scar start, the vanished

Ones peeled and singed the sacred
Inner skin, then mashed and boiled
Poultices from its healing bark.

Oh, lungs of the Earth, be praised.

The sound of running water's what I love.
The sound of running water soothes
The soul. What music it makes.

Turned fifty-four on Sun Mountain.
At forty-five my heart was sere,
A riverbed run dry. All it took was
A Sun Mountain day or two
To find the place again where water
Comes together in my middle. Now
I lay my head on rills, cleanse my ears
Dipping my body in living water.
All that dust sick and thick as sin,
Nearly gone now.

Docile, the soft supple thing
Subdues the hardest thing:
Water on stone
Beat against my heart
So all that's stone within me
Will loosen, dissolve.

I rub my beak on the smooth
Scar of a spirit tree's stripped
Bark, praying for a story
That will transform us,

Will heal the wounds
We've carved and carry.

Oh, lungs of the Earth, be praised.

In a hole notched in the tree
I see a poem pinned on a prayer flag,
A local recipe for medicine making:
Peel the inner bark of Ponderosa
Pine. Mash and mix with sap
Cook it up and eat.
Bless the Great Maker.
Bless Mother Earth.
    Be well.

Waking jays with their foolish chatter
Overwhelm me. All I want is to secret
Myself in an abandoned hiker's hut.
But then I spot the blood bright glow
Of plump chokecherries bending
A burning bush to earth below
As the light that fills the world
Breaks on sawtooth crags.

Tava's rising from the darkness,
Crimsons and purples the crest.

Clouds pinked and blued
Take a morning bath in ancient
Alpine lakes. Whoever doubted I'd
Shake the world's dust off my feet
And scale the eastern slope,
I proved them wrong.

Though I go sometimes hirpling,
Instead of soaring, and sometimes

Hopping instead of gliding, I go
Singing gladly along the Way.

The elders say the mountain's dying,
That *Tava* travels the path of all
Creation, goes the way of ripe
And rot, for *Tava* grows and flows
Then fades in time like sacred trees,
Rocks and springs, all things will
Slip someday under a new Niobraran Sea.

The Elders say cherish *Tava*.
Seeing how she settles into grains
Of sand. So sing *Tava*'s praise,
Smile knowing the mountaintop,
Like your dry and thirsty bone house,
Will dip beneath the rising waters.

The self-conscious critic in me was howling,
Cackling at my poems for sounding clunky.
Two stresses here won't do. This line wants more
Beats. You know nothing when it comes to counting
Measures. You toss in words that don't belong.
I laugh back, Mr. Critic, when you put
Your bookish life into words it sounds
Like a blind man singing about the sun.

The Path can't be mapped
Or seen. From time out of mind,
The Way comes and goes.
So now I know, climbing
Slow and sure up *Tava*
This is the real work,
The only work that lasts forever.

I've seen the old world's seven wonders,
Climbed the highest peaks.
Adoring spaces where water comes
Together, I sailed a hundred bays,
Rafted confluences of mighty rivers,
Kissed generals' asses, rubbed elbows
With ambassadors. But have I really seen
Anything, seen into the heart of things?
Who would have ever guessed
I'd end up sitting beneath a bent pine,
Squandering days, hands clasped around my
Knees, whispering praise to the cold silence?

Below myriad clouds,
Beside a slew of creeks,
Here dwells an idle, happy bird,
Sunning in *Tava*'s light, hopping
And flitting over folded, emerald
Foothills, rising daily at dusk,
Riding a thermal to sleep
In a hoodoo crevice till noon
Or a cave in mountain's middle.

Springs and falls run swiftly,
Though my heart races no longer.
Calm now, no more heart murmurs
Or self-deception. It's good to know
I need no flimsy crutch to hold me
Up, to steady me in raging streams.

The flows in fall are kind and slow now.
Autumn streams pool in quiet places.

ACKNOWLEDGMENTS

My debts run long and deep.

I am grateful to my editor Ellen Foos and Arlene Weiner at Ragged Sky Press for believing in my collection. Special thanks to Pamela Schnitter for working her design magic. To Steve Nolan for introducing me to Ragged Sky, championing my work, and becoming my brother.

I owe the greatest debt of gratitude to my best listener/reader/friend—my wife, Katie McGuire, you're the one, my only one, the soul who sets me straight when things get out of true.

Magpie no doubt deserves a full-throated shout out.

As these poems appeared, draft after draft, I relied on the keen eyes and capable ears of many remarkable writers and readers to help me hammer individual poems into a unity. Many of the same folks did heavy lifting and helped shape the collection into a more coherent image of magpiety.

Profound gratitude goes out to these incredible writers and mentors who read different versions of the manuscript front to back many times, and made it sing when it wasn't—Brian Turner, Donald Anderson, H.C. Palmer, Nat Anderson, Jim Bishop, Gary Mills.

In praise and thanksgiving for the life of Jonathan McGregor, my poet friend and first reader who left us far too soon—brother, you were there at the start. I know you're well and whole now. Wish you could have seen the final form of this thing we made strange together, this creature you helped me imagine from its earliest stages.

One of my aims was to fashion a kind of cabinet of curiosities, a museum of the murderous and miraculous. I couldn't have pursued and approached that goal without the contributions of three incredibly gifted and generous visual artists: Pam Aloisa, Benjamin Busch, and Moira McGuire. You each deserve the title *il miglior fabbor*.

To Lawrence McGuire (brother, artist, writer)—you taught me more about beauty than you'll ever know. Thanks for helping me learn how to sort the keepers from the crud.

To three amigos who've given wise counsel since they were captains: Jesse Goolsby, Brandon Lingle, Sean Purio. Officers, gentlemen, artists extraordinaire, unwavering friends—all three of you.

At different stages over the past two decades, the following friends, readers, and supporters have helped this book come into being: Katey Schultz, David Mason, Sarah Nance, Hugh Martin, Steve Nolan, David Haven Blake, Sean Purio, Ross Gresham, David Buchanan, Lori Davis-Perry, Tom Coakley, John Whittier-Ferguson, Kathleen Harrington, Murf Clark, Steve Legrand, Steve McCarty, Sonja Pasquantonio, Todd Chapman, Russ McDonald, Kyle Torke, Tom Hockel, Will Hughes, Ed McFadden, John Maxwell, Peter Balam, David Odom, David Jannetta, Charlanne Burke, Alpha Gunn.

Thanks to all the editors who believed in my work and for publishing earlier versions of the following:

"Three Ways of Looking at Magpie," "Every Bone Must Find Its Fellow Bone," and "Magpie Rises by Coming Down to Earth" appeared first in the journal *Dispatches from The Poetry Wars*, April 2020, and later in the anthology *Poetics for the More-Than-Human World* (Spuyten Duyvil, 2020).

A version of "Three Ways of Looking at Magpie" appeared as "Four Ways of Looking at Magpie—A Most Becoming Bird" in *Best New Poets 2020* (Samovar Press/Meridian, 2020).

Versions of "Runic Riddle," "Haggis," "Holding Still Becoming Magpie," "Gertrude Stein on A Soul's Miraculous Migration to Magpiety," "Artemis Goes Hunting," and Sections 1 & 2 of "Feeder off Battlefields" appeared in *Open-Eyed, Full-Throated: An Anthology of American/Irish Poets* (Syracuse UP, 2019).

An earlier version of "A Prayer for T.H., My Magpie, & Me" appeared in *Poetry While You Wait: An Anthology of Pikes Peak Poets* (Ed. Aaron Anstett, 2009).

"Heirloom Photograph" appeared in *War, Literature, & the Arts*, 22: 1&2 (2010).

"Het Huis" appeared in *The North American Review*, 293.2 (March-April 2008).

An earlier version of "Artemis Goes Hunting" appeared in *Revival Poetry Journal* Vol 10 (2009).

"Garden Plots" appeared in *War, Literature & the Arts*, 19: 1&2 (2007).

Versions of "Ghorban" and segments from "Feeder off Battlefields" appeared in a sequence poem entitled "Friends from Other Wars: Four Transcreative Translations," *War, Literature, & the Arts*, 17: 1 & 2 (2005).

"Peace Lily (with Peace Walls Leading to a Haiga)" appeared in *The Ekphrastic Review*, April 4, 2022.

"Ubi Sunt" appeared in *River Heron Review*, 4.2.

Thanks especially to *RHR* editors (Robbin Farr, Judith Lagana, Dawn Terpstra) for believing in "*Snag Breac* at Glendalough, Co. Wicklow," which won the 2022 *River Heron Review* Poetry Prize (*River Heron Review*, 5.2).

Special thanks to the following:

Brian T—you carried the manuscript all over the world & told me it was ready. Brother, you brighten our lives with your beauty and goodness.

Ross G—you steered me through the dark.

Donald—couldn't ask for a better friend/mentor: you pushed me to excellence, showed up for my ablation, gifted me the journal. Priceless gifts.

H.C.—you helped me see there's nothing like magpie out there. You and Val are the greatest.

Nat—you welcomed me into Open-Eyed, Full-Throated and listened when I was just starting out.

Ben B—leader, artist, friend in every sense of the word.

I've always connected the joy of poetry to its roots within oral tradition, public performance, and communal sharing. I've been blessed to live and work in many environments and communities that support these forms of poetic expression. In these spaces, I've received invaluable feedback and encouragement from people dedicated to the practice of poetry, the work of the humanities, and the pursuit of the arts. Chief among these have been gifted and generous poets in the Open-Eyed, Full-Throated poetry community at the American Conference for Irish Studies (Nat Anderson, Dan Tobin, Ed Madden, Eamon Wall, Drucilla Wall, Lawrence Welsh, David Lloyd, Adrian Rice, Kathryn Kirkpatrick, Renny Golden, Tyler Farrell, Christine Casson, Brendan Corcoran, Rand Brandes, T.D. Redshaw, James Silas Rodgers, Heather Bryant, Patrick Hicks, Joseph Lennon, Roslyn Blyn-LaDrew, Seamus Scanlon, Thomas O'Grady, Ann Neelon, Ray McManus, and Mary Madec).

A formative week spent in Gatlinburg, TN, at the Arrowmont School of Arts and Crafts as a Pentaculum 2017 Writer-in-Residence produced many of the earliest drafts of the poems here. Thanks to Katey Schultz for believing in me and for the invite. Thanks also to these Pentaculum writers-in-residence for their kindness, generosity of spirit, and sage advice: Van Jordan, Holly Wren Spaulding, Cameron Scott.

In the many places I've taught, studied, and written, dozens of colleagues have shaped both this project and my growth as a poet. Without the support of the Department of English and Fine Arts (DFENG) at the U.S. Air Force Academy (USAFA), this book would not exist. From Brig Gen (ret) Jack Shuttleworth's earliest belief in my promise as a teacher/writer to Col Tom Bowie's support of my English Ph.D. studies, I've always had supportive leaders. Chief among these: Col Candice Pipes, Col Dave Buchanan, Brig Gen (ret) Kathleen Harrington (Kathleen and Col Neal Barlow made the impossible possible by persuading the Air Force to release me for a six-month Fulbright Fellowship in Ireland). Brig Gen (ret) Jim Cook—you were always there cheering my work. To Lt Col (ret) Jim Meredith—thanks brother!

Inexpressible gratitude is due to my DFENG colleagues, especially the many long-time Works-In-Progress collaborators over the years: Tom Vargish, Col Kathleen Harrington, Don Anderson, Col Tom Coakley, Lori Davis Perry, Col Candice Pipes, Claudia Hauer, Col Liz Mathias, Jay Moad, Col Jim Cook, Andrea Van Nort, Col Dave Buchanan, Gary Mills, Col Jeff Collins, Richard Lemp, Fred Kiley, Bill Newmiller, Dale Ritterbusch, Katie Witt, Lindsay Zeller, Megan Kahn, Greg Laski, Richard Johnston, Ross Gresham, Daniel Couch, Mark Kaufman, Dave Lawrence, Edie Disler, José Antonio Arellano, Nicole Jerr, Melody Pugh, Sarah Nance, Gina Iberri-Shea, Hugh Martin, Alyssa Revels, Doug Cunningham, Jim Bishop, Steven Olsen-Smith, James Bishop, Greg Dandeles,

Joshua Hamm, Moranda Humphreys, Denys Van Renen, Kreg Abshire, Diana Polley, Darya Warner, Jessica Lopez, Amy Cooper, Pam Aloisa, Elisa Cogbill-Seiders, Max Sater, Mark Napolitano, Brittney Szempruch, Justin Newton, David Jorgenson, Sean Purio, Max Frazier, Betsy Muenger, Bill Weaver, Bill Mullen, Mike Sukach, Michelle Ruehl, Laurie Lovrak, John Farley, Don Zimmerman, Chris Campbell, Jim Meredith, Wilson Brissett, Allison Trueblood, Kate Schifani, Nate Hall, Rebecca Layng, Leah Young, Bridget Sharlow, Caroline Hampshire, Kyrstal McGuiness.

Several of these poems germinated during a Fulbright Fellowship at Mary Immaculate College (MIC, Limerick). I cherish the hospitality and support of MIC colleagues Eugene O'Brien and John McDonagh.

It was at readings with the Limerick White House Poets group I started hearing stirrings of my own voice among all the polyphonic magpie mimicry and masking that mark some of my poems. Thank you, Dominic Taylor and Barney Sheehan for giving new poets like me a stage. Thanks for fostering a vibrant, welcoming creative community.

My deepest gratitude to the many mentors and teachers along the way who gave me the gift of poetry—those who schooled me in the jurisdiction of form and the discipline of close reading—Ann Arbor (Linda Gregerson, John Whittier Feguson, George Bornstein, Simon Gikandi, Lawrence Goldstein); Sacramento (David Madden); San Francisco (Erasmo Leiva-Merikakis, Cornelius Buckley, S.J., John and Elisabeth Gleason), Innsbruck (Stan Arroyabe, Gudrun Grabher); Auburn (Mike Duda, Mark Underwood, Margaret Woodhouse, Laurie Maxson).

To my earliest teachers in the art of living and loving: my parents (Bev & Del) and my siblings (Terry, Leslie, and Larry).

Finally, to my *ecclesia domestica* (Katie, Kelsey, Dylan, Brigid, Seamus, Liam, Kieran & Moira). You're all saints for putting up with me and sacrificing so much as I pursued my poetry dream. You're all priceless gifts. Thank you, to put it simply, for everything.

Afterword: For an Abandoned Bird—I owe a parting debt of gratitude to a particular magpie chick, a near fledgling I almost crushed under foot some thirty years ago. One day in 1997, I stepped from my back door into a crystalline Colorado summer morning and discovered the castaway. I certainly would've killed him had he not been squawking at my feet.

There was nothing to do but rescue and nurse the scrawny magpie. With a medicine dropper, my kids and I fed the chick slimy, chopped worms grubbed from the good green earth. The bird survived, even seemed to thrive. But he showed no interest in learning to fly. After a week of his stubborn refusals, I decided to cloak the little man in a towel and commenced lofting him into the air. He flapped halfheartedly, barely managing to stay aloft for more than a second. After each failed sortie, the exhausted little bird looked utterly defeated. So went the first couple dozen flying lessons over the span of two days. On the third day, the bird somehow managed to fly about a meter. Then twelve, twenty, forty feet. I eventually placed him in the crook of a ponderosa bough. He raucously launched a full-throated infant version of the magpie chattering call—then he flew away.

I count that one of the better days in my early career as a father. We gave the magpie a new chance at life; he gave us so much more. What my kids learned from our magpie was a kind of care ethic that they'd carry through life and hand on to their children. Since that lucky morning in 1997, many sightings of magpies in both the natural world and cultural artifacts have taught me the *Pica* genus is supremely worthy of our attention and assent. You might say I've come to love magpies. What is love, after all, but giving something one's full, unfailing attention?

Has the world ever seen another bird worthy of such love? Probably. Yet, I'm immensely grateful that little magpie hopped into my life and inspired my magpie obsession. Grateful, too, for the way that abandoned bird initiated us, all those years ago, into the mystery of magpiety.

NOTES

Du muBt dein Leben ändern: Rilke's famous line, which is usually translated as "you must change your life," serves as this poem's title.

Runic Riddle: Who Am I? Answer: H I G O R A (magpie). This loose translation of the Old English is a modernized version of Riddle 24 in the *Book of Exeter,* one of the runic riddles. A literal translation of the final lines in the source text reads, "They name me *Giefu*, likewise *Ac* and *Rad*. *Os* supports me, *Hægl* and *Is*. Now I am called this just as these six staves clearly betoken." The runes spell H I G O R A, magpie (or jay). My mention of magpie being drunk ("sauced") refers to the magpie's association with Dionysus, the god of wine.

Alexander Wilson's Essential Magpie: A versified riff on the entry for magpie in Alexander Wilson's *American Ornithology* (1808).

Snag Breac at Glendalough, Co. Wicklow: In modern Irish the word for magpie is *snag breac*. In precolonial Ireland, *snag breac* denoted the greater spotted woodpecker, which went extinct in Ireland in the 1600s following the devastating deforestation of the country that accompanied colonization. In the late 1600s, a bird species previously unknown to the Irish, the magpie, migrated to Ireland from England. Native Irish speakers conferred the name *snag breac* on the new avian arrivals; *snag breac* lives on.

On Seeing a Jakhodo Scroll Painting: The type of Korean folk art paintings that inspired this poem is referred to as "Jakhodo." The character "jak" means magpie; "ho" means tiger; and "do" means painting. The inspiration for the events that unfold in the poem derives from *Kkachi horangi*, satirical paintings depicting magpies and tigers, a prominent motif found in the *minhwa* (folk art) of the Joseon period. In *kkachi horangi* paintings, the tiger, which is intentionally given a ridiculous appearance (hence its nickname "idiot tiger" 바보호랑이), represents authority and the aristocratic *yangban*, while the dignified magpie represents the common man. These paintings satirized the hierarchical structure of Joseon's feudal society.

Feeder off Battlefields: Sections 3 and 4 of this poem derive from a sequence of translated poem fragments which appeared in *War, Literature, & the Arts* under the title "Friends From Other Wars." Section 3 adapts found prose penned by Gustave Thibon in Le Peguy, occupied France, 1941. Section 4 riffs on fragments loosely modeled on a George Seferis war poem.

A Ripe Rude Garden: One historian of the American West performed the following unofficial tally of all reported kills recorded in the journals of Lewis and Clark, a document that reads like a catalogue of killing: 1,001 deer, 35 elk, 227 bison, 62 pronghorns, 113 beaver, 104 geese and brant, 48 shorebirds ("plovers"), 46 grouse, 45 ducks and coots, and 9 turkeys, 43 grizzly bears, 23 black bears, 18 wolves, and 16 otters. What the scholar omitted, however, was at least one noted magpie kill and the slaying of two Blackfeet Indian boys, one of whom (Side Hill Calf) had a Jefferson peace medal placed around his neck, *post mortem*, by Captain Lewis.

Three Ways of Looking at Magpie—A Most Becoming Bird: The Corps of Discovery journal entries which serve as the documentary basis for this poem are altered only in a dozen or so instances when versification invites or sometimes requires changes to the original text. That Lewis and Clark admired *pica hudsonia's* beauty is made clear by the pains they took crafting long journal passages that describe magpies in loving, intricate detail. Ironically, such passages are often followed by entries describing efforts to kill, capture, cage, and catalogue magpies—usually in the interest of advancing scientific knowledge.

Every Bone Must Find Its Fellow Bone: During their journey, Lewis and Clark sent back to "civilization" many specimens of natural history (both living and dead). Among these were a marmot and four living magpies, which Lewis and Clark sent as gifts to President Thomas Jefferson. Only one of the magpies reached Jefferson alive. Upon receiving this shipment of specimens from the Corps of Discovery, President Jefferson sent the marmot and the surviving magpie to Charles Willson Peale for his Philadelphia Museum, which housed and displayed a large collection of botanical, biological, and archaeological specimens. Peale's museum featured numerous live models, "vibrant specimens," from the Territories, including living birds such as magpies and Native American people. Peale wrote several letters to Thomas Jefferson on the magpies and other specimens received from Lewis and Clark (this poem draws from and creatively combines material contained in letters dated 3 Nov, 1805 and 12 Jan, 1806).

The Raising of the Dead: My liberal reworking of the Arapaho myth is magpied from Edward Curtis's controversial, yet invaluable ethnographic documentary account, *The North American Indian.* Despite its highly problematic status as an authentic record of Native American life and culture, N. Scott Momaday says of *The North American Indian,* "Taken as a whole, the work of Edward S. Curtis is a singular achievement."

Becoming Magpie: Section 3 highlights the capacity magpies have for recognizing themselves in a mirror. Many ornithologists and cognitive scientists note that mirror self-recognition has been demonstrated in European magpies, making them one of only a few species to possess this capability. Adrian McKinty notes that the Eurasian magpie's nidopallium is approximately the same relative size as those in chimpanzees and humans. The bird's total brain-to-body mass ratio is equal to most great apes and cetaceans, placing magpies among some of the most intelligent of all animals. In magpies, intelligence is indicated by tool use (language being one of the most sophisticated tools), an ability to hide and store food across seasons, episodic memory, using their own experience to predict the behavior of conspecifics. Another demonstrative behavior indicating intelligence: magpies cut their food in correctly sized proportions for the size of their young. In captivity, magpies have been observed counting to get food, imitating human voices, and regularly using tools to clean their own cages. In the wild, they organize themselves into gangs to pester coyotes and other competitors, and they use complex strategies hunting other birds (when insect food is scarce) as well as when confronted by predators.

Perhaps One World…but Please Not One Word for Bird: Across the globe, magpies have been unjustly accused of causing declines in songbird populations. Most biologists and ornithologists dispute such claims. Domesticated and feral cats kill between one to four billion birds a year in the lower forty-eight states. Whatever explains falling bird numbers, the rapid decline in bird populations is a clarion call for immediate and radical conservation efforts. Equally disturbing is the rate at which languages are going extinct: one language disappears every two weeks, a rate which exceeds the rate of bird extinctions.

Photograph on page 51: An image of Cheyenne Chief Magpie (Mo'ē'ha) who was born to Big Man and Magpie Woman, of Stone Calf's band, about 1851. Some historians argue Mo'ē'ha was present at the Sand Creek Massacre in 1864. He would have been around thirteen at the time. At age seventeen, Mo'ē'ha fought against American cavalry soldiers when George Custer and his troops attacked a snowbound Cheyenne encampment at Washita Creek in 1868, murdering as many as fifty innocent Cheyenne women and children by some accounts. On June 17, 1876, Mo'ē'ha again faced off against American cavalry soldiers at the battle of Rosebud (where Magpie was wounded twice by General Cook's troops). A week later, Mo'ē'ha joined in the Battle of the Little Bighorn, which resulted in the death of George Custer. On multiple occasions, then, Mo'ē'ha thwarted attempts by Custer and other American troops to kill him. Mo'ē'ha died in his sleep in Oklahoma on March 16, 1931. A case study in survivance, Chief Magpie's story should be a touchstone in the annals of Western American history. It is a story, however, that has largely been kept out of the history books. Photograph courtesy of Oklahoma Historical Society and Mark L. Gardner, who was given the photo from the private collection of Oklahoma author Charles J. Brill.

Force, the Hero: This poem loosely and liberally adapts translated fragments from Homer's epic and the essay *"L'Iliade*, ou Le Poème de la Force" by Emile Novis (pseudonym of Simone Weil), written in Paris during the summer and fall of 1940 after the Nazis occupied France. The version of Weil's essay used for my translation/adaptation appeared in *Les Cahiers du Sud*, 1 décembre 1940, 561-574.

Magpie Sings on Sun Mountain: The cultures and places which gave rise to the ancient mythopoeic songs behind this sequence (the Chinese *Cold Mountain* poems and the Old Irish *Buile Suibhne*) couldn't be more distant from each other, but what the poems and the mad poets at the heart of each of these ancient poems hold in common is a shared sense of the value inherent in the life of poetry and the wholeness granted by a life lived in closer accord with the salubrious slow rhythms of the natural world. Ecopoetics and ecopo-ethics are clearly not new concepts. The laughing hermit poet Han Shan found enlightenment on Cold Mountain. The bird-man Suibne Geilt found peace in the sacred grove of Ulster's Glen Bolcan.

In this poem, I use the Nuuchiu (Ute) word for Pikes Peak in Colorado, *Tava-kaavi*, (Sun Mountain). The word *Tava* denotes both the star at the center of our solar system and the easternmost 14,115-foot peak on the Front Range. Vision seekers have long sought sanctuary on the slopes of

Tava. According to two Nuuchiu spokespersons from the Southern Ute Cultural Affairs Department (Garrett Briggs and Cassandra Atencio), the Utes were likely the first people to ascend the mountain and its foothills for ceremonial and practical purposes. The nomadic forbears of present-day Utes, the Ancestral Nuuchiu visited the peak from time immemorial on their annual circuit through Colorado's mountains, high-country parks, and plains. As a signifier for a sacred mountain and the sun, *Tava* is a word redolent with sacred meaning according to Dr. James Jefferson, a Southern Ute elder and linguist. Indeed, a version of the Utes's creation story says their ancestors were fashioned from twigs contained in a bag and dropped by Coyote at the mountain's base. There the Nuuchiu could be closer to their Creator. The tree twigs spouted limbs and heads and became human. This story reminds us how, in some indigenous cultures, the borders separating humans and plants and animals have sometimes been far less rigid, far more porous. Restoring a viable sense of our place in nature and healing the life-threatening wounds we've inflicted upon our planet will no doubt demand a much deeper sense of shared experience (indeed our kinship) with the animal, mineral and vegetable worlds. My turn towards the more-than-human world begins with the merger I make with Magpie.

ILLUSTRATION CREDITS

"Magpie Thicket," cover image watercolor by Pam Aloisa, © 2024.
"Tiger and Magpie," drawing by Moira McGuire, © 2024.
"Bird Man," drawing by Moira McGuire, © 2024.
"Magpie," drawing by Benjamin Busch, © 2024.
1930 photograph of Cheyenne Chief Mo'ē'ha (Magpie), courtesy of Oklahoma Historical Society and Mark L Gardner (with permission).
"Lizard," drawing by Benjamin Busch, © 2024.
"Lily of Peace," painting by Pam Aloisa, © 2022.
"Rock Wall," drawing by Benjamin Busch, © 2024.

ABOUT THE AUTHOR

Thomas McGuire is a poet, translator, essayist, and literary critic. He was raised in Northern California (yellow-billed magpie country). Now he makes his home in Colorado (black-billed magpie range). Since 1995 he's taught at the U.S. Air Force Academy, where he's a Professor of English. He's the editor of *War, Literature & the Arts*. His creative and scholarly publications have appeared in journals and anthologies such as *The North American Review, Best New Poets 2020, Zocalo Public Square, New Hibernia Review, Poetics for the More-Than-Human World, The Ekphrastic Review*, and *Open-Eyed, Full-Throated: An Anthology of American/Irish Poets*. In 2008, he was a Fulbright Scholar to Ireland. In 2014, he concluded a twenty-four-year Air Force career. He writes in the rain shadow of the mountain the Utes call *Tava* (Sun Mountain). *Dark Devouring* is his first collection.

www.ingramcontent.com/pod-product-compliance
Lightning Source LLC
Chambersburg PA
CBHW051606170426
43196CB00038B/2950